The Life and Times

of

MOONDYNE JOE

Swan River Colony Convict,

JOSEPH BOLITHO JOHNS

by

W.J. Edgar

The Life and Times

of

MOONDYNE JOE

Swan River Colony Convict,

JOSEPH BOLITHO JOHNS

by

W.J. Edgar

Published jointly

by

Tammar Publications

and the

Toodyay Tourist Centre

Jacket Design by P & S Graphics, Mt Hawthorn
Typeset by The Type Foundry, Osborne Park
Printed by Eastern Press, Osborne Park

ISBN   0 646 00047 0

In memory of
Bert Chitty and Arny Hutchings,
West Toodyay men
who loomed large during my formative years.

CONTENTS

INTRODUCTION

Each and every one of the 162,000 felons who came to Australia as convicts lived a 'pre-life' in Britain or Ireland before stepping aboard a convict transport - a life which tells us much about the society from which they came, its iniquities and injustices; how it shaped the attitudes of the convicts before transportation. Naturally these factors had powerful impacts on the early days of the colonies and, conceivably, strong influences in helping shape our attitudes and perspectives in Australia today.

Therefore, rather than just look at the career that Moondyne Joe led after arrival in the Swan River Colony in 1853, let's go back further to the places of his childhood and adolescence, build up a picture of his early years as best we can, and attempt to ascertain how his formative years before transportation might have influenced his attitudes and actions after coming ashore from the "Pyrenees" at Fremantle.

Joe's life has been coloured by the popular press over the years to the point where he is largely regarded, variously, as villainous ruffian, a petty gangster or just a buffoon. That is superficial and unfair. It would seem there is much more to him than that.

One hundred and fifty years ago life was extremely hard for the lower classes in Britain. But it was also around this time that the 'lower orders' had begun to agitate strongly for a better deal. Organisations like the Luddites and the Chartists (manhood suffrage, vote by ballot, equal electoral districts, annual parliaments, no property qualifications for members of parliament and payment of parliamentary members) were growing and beginning to flex their muscles, much to the chagrin of the controlling, propertied classes.

Youngsters like Joe would probably have been increasingly aware of the iniquities that existed. It is very likely he suffered, like many others, the often callous disregard by the mine and factory owners.

So rather than just classify Joe as just a clown or an unthinking villain it would be more balanced to examine the other side of the coin and attempt to find out how much he might have been influenced by the new wave of agitation for social justice.

His later actions hint at it. He fought the authorities with a degree of determination which seem to go beyond mere contrariness. He was difficult and 'artful' (the authorities' description) to an uncommon degree and despite tremendous pressure to cow and subdue him he remained obdurate until, eventually, they relented, realising there was little point in continuing his incarceration. In the end Joe defeated the system, but at what price?

Was he, in fact, rather than an unthinking rascal from the wrong side of the tracks, something of a social pioneer, believing in the rightness of his cause and extremely angry at the treatment meted out by one sector of the community on another? Or is that carrying it too far? His actions were more intuitive than deliberate, perhaps, but nevertheless an influence which the authorities could not control or quash and, in the end, they relented.

But it is really for YOU to decide. Hopefully the material within these covers will help shed new light and new perspectives on Joe. Perhaps, then, he will become something more than the shallow two-dimensional figure that, in the main, has thus far been portrayed.

PROLOGUE:

Convicts Arrive in the Swan River Colony

Why convicts at the Swan River in 1850 anyway, when the earliest settlers had vowed it would remain a 'free labour' colony?

The fact is it didn't take the first colonists very long at all to perceive the difficulties they were in and realise what might face them for many years to come. R.M. Lyon wrote to the Secretary of State for the Colonies as early as February, 1831 stating that, ".... the settlers to a man have changed their opinion since they encamped within the shores of Australia .... A settler .... said to me: 'I came here because no convicts were to be sent, but so completely are my sentiments altered on the subject that if a petition for convict labour were moved tomorrow, I should be ready to put my name to it.'" (1) That just 20 months after the colony had first been settled.

A petition from a body of settlers at King George's Sound (Albany) was sent to the Secretary of State in 1834 through Governor Stirling. Perhaps many of the signatories had been in Albany while the contingent of N.S.W. convicts was still there (a convict settlement had been established at King George's Sound under the auspices of the Government of N.S.W. in December, 1826 and withdrawn in 1831). It seems the Albany colonists were undaunted by a possible re-introduction.

Though the petition conceded the colony was set up under a system of free labour they maintained, ".... that forced labour was necessary to open up proper lines of communication between various settlements .... They were persuaded that the country was not deficient in natural possibilities, but .... in the absence of a market the settler had no inducement to labour (saw no reason to work hard for so little gain).

The only remedy was the introduction of convicts. Failing that they felt the settlement could only advance at the sacrifice of the first settlers and their entire capital .... the wisdom of the majority of settlers and (by contrast) of the Home authorities (and James Stirling) may be questioned in the light of events of less than 15 years afterwards, when at the request of the colonists generally convicts were introduced to carry out the same policy of construction and development that was urged at this time (1834), and which would have been of such inestimable value to the settlers of those early days." (2)

But, for the moment, the early settlers, imbued by the principle of free labour through the strong conservative elements within the administration, struggled on.

By the mid-40s the availability of any labour was virtually non-existent. In 1845 departures by sea from the colony exceeded the numbers coming in. One must assume many of those who left were skilled artisans or labourers. "Without labour - forced or free - development was almost impossible." (3)

In the previous year, 1844, a general meeting of the York Agricultural Society had formulated a motion urging that the Home Government and the Secretary of State do something about the labour problems. The motion was not put but a committee sought out Governor Hutt and discussed the problem with him. They received no encouragement but public debate was re-kindled, though it was limited. The all important newspaper support was only lukewarm too. Additionally a body of opinion existed which maintained that the introduction of convicts would harm the credibility of the colony and very much hinder moves toward eventual self-government.

In January 1846, W.S. Stockeley, the manager of Frederick Mangles and Co., forwarded to the Secretary of State a long petition urging the introduction of convicts to W.A.. By the beginning of 1847 Stockeley's memorial was receiving widespread support. Even the papers were changing their tune. They saw advantages in cheap labour and an invigorated public works programme. But the Perth Gazette suggested: ".... the convicts should be confined in hulks, not allowed to mix with free people, and returned to England when their services were no longer required." (4) The high principled ideals on which the colony had been founded were dying hard.

But the governor would not support the idea. "At the opening of the Legislative Council in June, 1847, he vehemently opposed the agitation and regretted that 'the dearth of labour or the desire to accumulate wealth on the part of a portion of the community had caused the suggestion to be entertained .....' He concluded by saying, "With the experience of other colonies before us, which we now witness struggling to free themselves from this system as from a pestilence, I would strongly urge all who are favourable to the measure to consider whether the injury likely to be entailed on the community, and particularly on their own families, may not convince them, when too late, that they have obtained their object at a dreadful sacrifice." (5)

There the matter languished until the arrival of Governor Fitzgerald toward the end of 1848. He had been instructed in London to find out on arrival whether the colonists would take prisoners who had served their mandatory separate confinement period in Pentonville. After investigation Fitzgerald was sufficiently encouraged (although the divisions of opinion within the colony were still considerable) to ask Earl Grey for a hundred ticket of leave men.

With this new impetus a public meeting was held in Perth on the 23rd February, 1849. Resolutions were laid before the governor with a request he forward them to the Secretary of State. (6)

Governor Fitzgerald concluded: "I am far from recommending Your Lordship to adopt this proposition, as few, I think, would from choice select a convict settlement as a residence for themselves and families; but in the present state of affairs here I must say that if Her Majesty's Government wish to establish another penal settlement in Australia the majority of the inhabitants would gladly learn that Western Australia was chosen as the site." (7)

Earl Grey (Secretary of State) proposed sending convicts having completed their separate confinement, that they should be confined (in W.A.) to particular districts and their passage money re-imbursed to the Treasury from wages earned. Otherwise they would be free.

On the 1st May, 1849 an Order-in-Council was passed nominating the Swan River Colony as a place to which convicts could be sent from the United Kingdom. A late decision by the Secretary of State calmed the fears of many still opposed to the scheme - he declared that an equal number of free settlers to convicts would be sent out. The convicts would be solely in the control of the government for employment on public works etc. They would only be available to colonists for labour when they were free from the building of public roads, bridges and buildings etc.

The first batch of 75 convicts arrived aboard the "Scindian" on the 1st June, 1850. "..... and thus the colony celebrated its twenty first birthday by assuming the character of an actual penal settlement." (8)

CHAPTER ONE:

Joseph Bolitho Johns

Joseph Johns was arraigned at the Brecon Assizes (central Wales) in March, 1849, along with John Williams (William Cross) on a charge of burglary and stealing (see Chapter Six, "CASE STUDIES" - John Williams)

Johns was an iron ore miner by trade (1) and that, allied with the fact that he was associated with Williams, a boatman on the Brecon to Monmouth canal serving the ironworks at Clydach - and also that he was tried in Brecon - probably meant the youngster lived in the approximate location of the Clydach Iron Works, which in those days, by necessity, was closeby the coalfields from which came the fuel to fire the ironworks furnaces. Whether Joe was born and raised in the area is problematical. His second name is of Cornish origin and there was, in fact, some migration between the Cornish mines and the Welsh valleys at the time.

It was not uncommon for children of eight or nine years of age to work in those primitive mine workings. Small of stature they could be sent into normally inaccessible 'drives'. Deaths from frequent accidents in the crude workings, and from diseases such as pnuemonia, phthisis and bronchitis, were common among the juvenile population of the central Welsh valleys. Undernourished, frail bodies would easily succumb to the multitude of hazards. (2)

To survive these conditions one had to be hardy and resourceful. Johns was to prove he was all of these in the years to come.

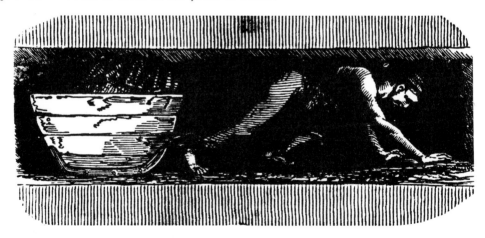

Here is a young boy pulling a sledge on which is a wooden tub full of coal. Around the boy's waist is a harness and from that running down between his legs and attached to the sledge is a chain. Examples of a sledge and a chain and a chain harness can be seen in the Mining Gallery at the National Museum of Wales.

It was Johns who seemed to have taken the initiative from the older Williams in their spirited defence at the Lent Assizes before the judge, Sir William Erle and the jury of 'peers'. But the newspaper report of the trial (The Welshman - 30th March 1849) hints that he was abrasive and contravened the conventions of court procedure. It was to cost him dearly.

Johns and Cross had already waited about four months for their case to be heard. They would have spent the cold, miserable winter of 1848-49 languishing in a cell or labouring on a government work party in the area. Neither option would have been comfortable in the least.

After the sentencing (ten years transportation) it took almost another seven months before they were lodged at Millbank in London, a holding prison opened in 1821 as the first national penitentiary with cells rather than large communal yards for prisoners, as had been the former practice (It had been maintained that prisoners had been learning more in prison than out of it - one observer records having seen a group of young boys blindfold themselves, form a ring and take it in turns to pick each others pockets). The cell system had been introduced, in part, to counteract this and a host of similar, dubious activities.

Johns and Williams were lodged in Pentonville prison on the 1st of January 1850, to begin their mandatory period of separate confinement.

THE PENTONVILLE SYSTEM:

The authorative thinking of the time was that each transgressor should be lodged in a cell and completely removed from the company of his former colleagues. It was reasoned that each prisoner could not be further tainted by others and, in solitude, would have ample time to reflect on the error of his ways. Hence the word, PENITENTIARY - probably derived from the latin, 'penitus' meaning, deep inside. From this root are derived other English words such as 'penance' which means: "a ..... discipline imposed by church authority" or "....punishment undergone in token for penitence of sin." (3) There are others such as penal and repent. And repent was exactly what was expected of each prisoner, or else!

The word 'cell' originally came from the monasteries. It was a monk's room where he could examine, in solitude, the depths of his soul. It was ordered by the authorities that the convicts do the same.

"Outside, the day may be blue and gold," said Oscar Wilde, "but the light that creeps down through the thickly-muffled glass of the small iron-barred window beneath which one sits is grey and niggard. It is always twilight in one's cell, as it is always midnight in one's heart." (4) This was the description of his cell at Reading gaol.

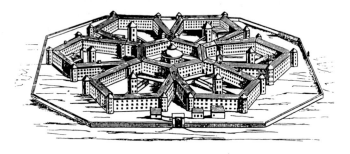

BIRD'S-EYE VIEW OF MILLBANK PRISON.
(Copied from a Model by the Clerk of the Works.)

As regards the details of the building itself, the following are the technical particulars:—

The prison occupies an area of 6 3/4 acres. It has "a curtain wall with massive posterns in front," where, as we have said, stands a large entrance gateway, the latter designed by Barry, whose arches are filled with portcullis work; whilst from the main building rises an "Italian" clock-tower. From the central corridor within radiate four wings, constructed after the fashion of spokes to a half-wheel, and one long entrance hall, leading to the central point. The interior of each of the four wings or "corridors" is fitted with 130 cells, arranged in three "galleries" or storeys, one above the other, and each floor contains some forty-odd apartments for separate confinement.

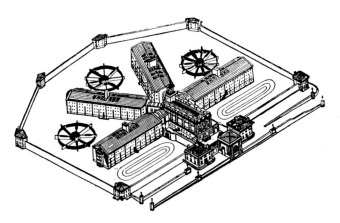

BIRD'S EYE VIEW OF PENTONVILLE PRISON.
(From Drawing in the Report of the Surveyor-General of Prisons.)

Every cell is 13 1/2 feet long by 7 1/2 feet broad, and 9 feet high, and contains an earthenware water-closet, and copper wash-basin, supplied with water; a three-legged stool, table, and shaded gas-burner—besides a hammock for slinging at night, furnished with mattress

* The total number withdrawn from separation in the year 1854 was 66, and 23 of these were put to work in association on mental grounds, consisting of cases in which men of low intellect began under separate confinement to exhibit mental excitement, depression, or irritability, whilst 12 more were removed to public works before the expiration of their term of separate confinement, because they were, in the words of the medical officer, "likely to be injuriously affected by the discipline of the prison." By a summary of a list of the cases requiring medical treatment—as given in the Medical Officer's Report of 1855—we find, that of the diseases, 35.9 per cent, consist of constipation, and 16.5 per cent of dyspepsia—the other affections being "catarrahs," of which the proportion is 20.7 per cent., and diarrhoea 10.0 per cent., whilst the remaining 16.9 per cent. was made up of a variety of trivial and anomalous cases.

Even during the hour-long exercise periods every day prisoners wore hoods so that they could not recognise friends. Complete silence was strictly enforced. During visits to the prison chapel inmates were segregated by partitioning so that they could see only the ministering chaplain at the altar in front of them.

These methods may very well have been effective for monks. Such men were undoubtedly motivated and were doing it of their own volition but, as time would tell, it had a very different affect on many of the convicts.

'In this isolated state, ... in the solitude of the cell ... alone with God and a wounded conscience, the unhappy man is forced to exercise his powers of reflection, and thus acquires a command over his sensual impulses which will probably exert a permanent influence.' (5)

For the Reverend J. Kingsmill, a further, but rather different attraction of 'solitary' was the nicety with which it was 'calculated to strike more terror into the minds of the lowest and vilest class of criminals than any other hitherto devised, whilst those who have not fallen so low, feel more than compensated for its peculiar pressure, by the protection and privacy which it affords, and most of all the penitent.' (6)

In 1842, when Pentonville penitentiary was first opened, the separate confinement period to be undergone by each prisoner was eighteen months. At the time Johns and Williams began their long, solitary vigil it had been reduced to twelve months - with good reason. There had been serious concern, stated in the sixth report of the Pentonville commissioners, that there were "some instances of partial aberration of mind not amounting to insanity," and "... the occurrence of hysterical convulsions in some of the convicts on their first being embarked for transportation." (7)

In 1853 the period of separate confinement was further reduced to nine months and then later to six months.

It appears very likely that Joseph Johns was an early victim. The records show that he was transferred to Shorncliffe on the 1st March, 1850 after only two months at Pentonville. Whatever the reason it must have been thought sufficiently serious by Mr Burt, the principal warder, the prison medical officer, the prison governor, Mr Chesterton, and the Reverend Kingsmill, prison chaplain, to have him taken him from Pentonville. (8)

Social reformer, Elizabeth Fry did not think much of the system. She remarked in her journal: "They may be building, though they little think it, dungeons for their children and their children's children, if times of religious persecution and political disturbance should return." (9)

Oscar Wilde had perhaps the most damning view: "As one reads history, not in the expurgated editions written for schoolboys and passmen, but in the original authorities of each time, one is absolutely sickened, not by the crimes that the wicked have committed, but by the punishments that the good have inflicted ...." (10)

Convicts Exercising at Pentonville

Shorncliffe was an army camp on high ground above Folkestone on the English channel. Work parties there would have been under the overall supervision of the army authorities and discipline was probably less stringent than that imposed at the prisons. The Reverend Mr Kingsmill, whose signature is in that particular column of the Pentonville register, may have had this in mind when he recommended Joe's removal on what, in part, may have been compassionate grounds.

Do all these factors point to what we might call today, a 'mental breakdown'? Certainly it is consistent with what occurred to many others. They simply could not 'take' the months of silence and solitude (It is interesting to note that most of the prisons built under the Pentonville pattern had lunatic asylums subsequently built closeby - e.g.:- the Fremantle asylum, now the Museum and Arts Centre in Parry Street). Does it also explain the irrationality of Johns's subsequent behaviour in Western Australia when he was put under similar pressures by the authorities?

Johns was transferred to Dartmoor prison from Shorncliffe and was admitted on the 21st October 1851. We can take another glimpse into the Johns persona via a glance at the Shorncliffe misconduct book encompassing the eighteen month period he was there. There are thirteen entries encapsulated perhaps by the single, illuminating one word comment at the end:- "ARTFUL". (11)

Johns didn't last long at Dartmoor prison. While his friend, John Williams, stayed to be transported to Van Dieman's Land early in the following year, Joe was returned to London and lodged aboard the convict hulk, "Justitia". It is very likely Joe had been 'playing up' again. At that particular time only the 'difficult' prisoners (and the incapacitated) were being placed aboard the hulks.

The 'separate system' in Pentonville's chapel.

Life aboard the hulks at Woolwich, anchored in the stench and filth of the Thames tidal mud flats, would not have been pleasant at all. Conditions, in fact, were abysmal.

The prisoners on the hulks were ferried daily to the military base and were put to work on a variety of tasks such as scraping shot, dredging mud and repairing buildings and facilities. They were subject to the strictest discipline and given classifications accordingly. As they progressed through the categories they moved closer to being placed on board a transport bound for one of the Australian colonies (see page 21).

When the "Justitia" was destroyed by fire Johns was placed aboard the "Defence" for the remainder of his time. (12) After a little over a year he was placed aboard the "Pyrenees" which sailed for the Swan River Colony on the 2nd of February 1853. It had been well over four years since his apprehension outside Chepstow in Wales.

This was unusual. Over the eighteen years of transportation to the Swan River Colony the majority of convicts had been incarcerated for shorter periods than that prior to embarkation. In the years, 1850/51, 80% had been in prison for 2-3 years; for 1861/62, 83% for 2-3 years and for the period 1866/68, 82.3% were imprisoned for 1-2 years (97.2% for 3 years or less). (13) Again this suggests that Joe may have been quite troublesome to the authorities. In consequence it took him longer than usual to accrue the necessary credit points to be placed aboard a transport ship (13).

It is difficult to imagine the privation, brutality, mental agony and anguish that Joseph Johns, and the many thousands like him, underwent during that time. One paid a heavy price indeed for what we would regard, in the latter half of the twentieth century, a minor offence.

The English Prison Hulks

When the American colonies ceased to be available after 1776 the justices in England, still with over 200 capital offences on the statute books, used the transportation method of sentencing liberally as the only alternative to hanging. And so there were thousands sentenced to transportation with nowhere to go. Parliament was at its wit's end.

Men were turned to labour, raising sand, soil and gravel and cleansing the Thames and other rivers. It was a new idea in English penal thinking - hard labour at home. (14)

The supervision of prisoners on works was left to the justices of Middlesex (London area) and they in turn sub-contracted overseers. Duncan Campbell bought old ships (the "Justitia"and "Censor") and anchored them in streams between Gallion's Reach and Barking Reach. Out of the contract monies they were to provide the prisoner's food and clothing too. Campbell received thirty eight pounds ($76) per man, per year. Out of this amount he was also to provide for officers and guards.

The Act of Parliament ratifying this arrangement received royal assent in May, 1776.

In the first two years 176 of the 632 prisoners died; in the third year there were even more deaths. It wasn't surprising. Conditions aboard were even worse than the very sub-standard London prisons.

Prisoners were put 'tween decks' en masse. It was overcrowded and foul odours permeated through the ship. A man had one rug and a 20 inch (51cm) X 6 foot (183cm) bed space. Six men slept on a platform which doubled as a table during the day. Despite regulations few washed or shaved and the clothing was of poor quality and fell apart quickly.

One ex-prisoner said: "Half the time they gave us provisions which the very dogs refuse .... the bread is not baked and is only good to bang against a wall. The meat looks as though it's been dragged in the mud for miles. If you refuse to eat it nothing is given in its place." (15)

The prisoners worked ten hours a day in summer and seven in winter. In other words they could be battened down in their freezing, filthy quarters for over 15 hours. Time hung heavy, gambling was rife and many escapes were planned.

" A rough code of honour existed ... but didn't prevent vice ..... There existed ... perverse immorality, shameful outrages, ... cynicism and inconceivable misery. Those that survived were strong and hard-bitten men. Sheer lack of food combined with gambling away clothing and personal possessions made them look like a generation of dead men rising for a moment from their tombs, hollow-eyed, wan and earthy of complexion; bent-backed, shaggy-bearded and of terrifying emaciation." (16)

The guards were the lowest class of human beings; devoid of feeling, ignorant, brutal, tyrannical and cruel. They carried large sticks and used them liberally.

The whole system was in fact uneconomical but it was very much cheaper than building new prisons. By 1783 the "Dunkirk" at Plymouth, the "Lion" at Gosport and the "Fortune" and "Ceres" at Langston Harbour had been set up as hulks.

By 1802 the hulks had become so notorious that the authorities were forced to appoint inspectors and improve some conditions. Newer and larger vessels were put into service and hospital ships were attached to each hulk depot. Food was improved, hammocks were issued and a chapel instituted on each ship.

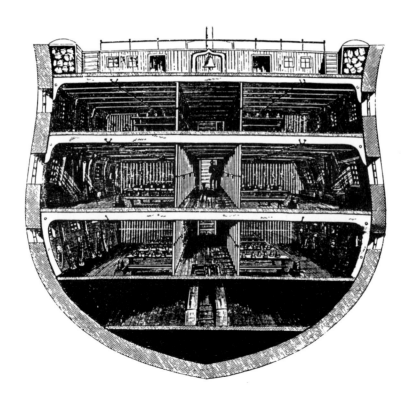

Section View of the Interior of the "Defence Hulk".

With prisoners arriving in England from the Napoleonic wars in considerable numbers, 60 hulks were in use by 1814. After 1811 separation had been instituted. Cells with 10-16 prisoners each were built and a passageway put down the middle so that guards could supervise more closely. It made an appreciable difference.

By 1828 there were only 10 hulks with 4446 prisoners aboard in England. The numbers decreased further until 1840 then increased again for three years as demand rose after transportation ceased to New South Wales.

There was a further enquiry into conditions aboard the hulks in 1847. In consequence the diet improved, the guards were increased and good conduct awards were instituted (see over). But of the 53,000 people who died in England and Wales in 1848 a disproportionate number were believed to have died aboard. This proportion was probably accentuated by the fact that after 1840 the healthier, better-behaved prisoners were lodged in Millbank. Only the weaker ones and the intransigents were left aboard the hulks.

After a series of riots and mutinies in the 1840s the worst types of criminals were moved to Gibraltar and Bermuda. By the time Joseph Johns began his terms on the "Justitia" at the end of 1852 conditions were better than they'd been before (particularly during the period of the Napoleonic Wars). But they were still far from good.

The most appalling conditions of all were at Bermuda in a much hotter climate than in England. "..... in the close and stifling nights of summer," wrote the Reverend J.M. Guilding in 1859, "the heat between the decks is so oppressive as to make the stench intolerable, and to cause the miserable inmates frequently to strip off every vestige of clothing and gasp at the portholes for a breath of air." (17)

Around two thousand convicts were usually kept at Bermuda, quartered at Saint George's and Ireland Island. They were principally employed by the Royal Navy erecting fortifications and other public works.

In the forty years between 1823 and 1861, 9094 convicts served in Bermuda. Of these 2041 died of disease ranging through tuberculosis, dysentary, yellow fever and delirium tremens. It was a horrifying rate of attrition.

* *Badges, &c.*–A distinctive portion of the discipline carried on at Woolwich consists in the badges worn by the prisoners on the left arm, and the rings worn on the right. These badges are made of black leather, with an edge of red cloth, with white and black letters and figures upon it. We advanced towards some convicts who were hauling up linen to the mast to dry, and who wore both rings and badges. The first badge we examined was marked thus:–

The 7 meant that the prisoner had been sentenced to *seven* year's transportation; the 8 that he had been in the hulk that number of months, and the V.g., that his conduct had been *very good* all the time he had been there. Another man wore a badge marked thus:–

<pre>
┌─────────────┐
│   4   │
│ G   6 │
│   8   │
└─────────────┘
</pre>

This denoted that the prisoner was suffering *four* year's penal servitude; that his conduct had been good during *six* months; and that he had been on board the hulk *eight* months.

These badges are collected once in every month, and conveyed to the governor's office. The character-book, as filled up from the weekly reports of the warders, is gone over in each case, and, at the same time, if the prisoner have behaved badly, his badge is altered, and he loses some advantages of his previous good conduct.* Three months' good report in the character-book constitutes a V.G. or *very good,* and advances the wearer three months towards the second stage of penal servitude. Accoringly the man's class is not marked upon his badge.

But the first man whose badge we noticed upon his left arm, had also upon his right arm a blue and two red rings. The blue ring denotes the second stage of penal servitude, and the red rings that he is a first-class convict. One red ring upon the right arm makes a second-class convict; and the third-class prisoner is known by the absence of all rings from his arm. by this system we are assured that it is almost impossible that a prisoner can be unjustly dealt with

* "The badges which are given as a record to the prisoner of his actual position with reference to character, have proved to be great encouragement; and that they are prized is evidenced by the efforts made to obtain them, and to regain them by good conduct in such cases as they may have been forfeited.

"The Governor of Portland Prison observes:–

"'The system of wearing conduct-badges on the dress, by which the monthly progress of each convict towards the attainment of his ticket-of-leave is publicly marked, works very satisfactorily, as is evinced by the anxiety of even the ill-conducted prisoners to regain a lost good-conduct mark, and the efforts to keep subsequently clear of the misconduct book.'

"As a means of promoting good conduct, a system of classification has also been adopted, the object of which will be best understood from the rules established with reference to it, which are as follows:–

"'The prisoners shall be divided into three classes, to be called the first, second, and third classes. the classification shall depend, in the first instance, on the report of character and general conduct since conviction that may be received with a prisoner; and subsequently, on his actual conduct, industry, and observed character under the discipline of the establishment.

"'6. Prisoners in either the first or second classes shall be liable to removal to a lower class for misconduct. The prisoners in the different classes shall be distinguished by badges, indicating the particular class to which each prisoner may belong.

"'7. Prisoners who habitually misconduct themselves will be liable to be sent back to separate confinement, or to be removed to some penal establishment under more severe discipline.

"'8. The object of the classification is not only to encourage regularity of conduct and a submission to discipline in the prison, by the distinctions that will be maintained in the different classes, but to produce on the mind of the prisoners a practical and habitual conviction of the effect which their own good conduct and industry will have on their welfare and future prospects.

"'9. Such distinctions shall be made between the classes, and such privileges granted, as shall promote the object of giving encouragement to those whose good conduct may deserve it, provided such distinctions do not interfere with discipline nor with the execution of a proper amount of labour on public works.'"–*Report on the Discipline and Construction of Portland Prison, and its Connection with the System of Convict Discipline now in operation, by* Lieut.-Col. Jebb, C.B., 1850.

The Reverend Guilding said about them (the hulks) in 1860 what many probably should have said years before: "..... these dens of infamy and pollution ... the great majority of the prisoners confined in the hulks become incurably corrupted, and that they leave them, in most cases, more reckless and hardened in sin than they were on reception .... Few are aware of the extent of suffering to which a prisoner is exposed on board the hulks, or of the horrible nature of the association by which he is surrounded. There is no safety for life, no supervision over the bad, no protection to the good .... They are productive of sins of such foul impurity and unnatural crime that one even shudders to mention them .... A mob law, a tyranny of the strong over the weak, exists below, which makes the well-disposed live in constant misery and terror." (18)

Hulks were finally abolished in England in 1857. It was a further five years before these 'hells on earth' were broken up in Bermuda. Most of the prisoners were sent back to England and re-assigned to other prisons or sent to the Swan River Colony (see CASE STUDY - convict, WILLIAM GENTLE).

The story of the prison hulks is one of the blackest episodes in eighteenth and nineteenth century English social history.

H.M.S. Warrior as a hulk at Woolwich, 1846.

CHAPTER TWO:

The Voyage, Arrival and Early Days in the Swan River Colony

THE VOYAGE:

The "Pyrenees" was owned by Duncan Dunbar who had been contracted by the British Government to transport the prisoners and stipulated cargo. The contractor was to supply, as usual, all the provisions.

Ship's captain was Benjamin Freeman. His loyalty was to his employer, the owner of the vessel. He would have had little proprietary interest in the personal well-being of the convicts other than to land them at their destination as quickly as possible. He would then hope to secure a return cargo either from Australia or India or Africa. In so doing a tidy profit could be made from the total voyage on behalf of the owners of the vessel.

The man who looked after the personal well-being of the convicts on behalf of Her Majesty's Government was the ship's surgeon - in this particular case, Dr John Bower.

For a young man keen to go to the Antipodes and perhaps seek his fortune it was a convenient way to travel. The passage was free and he was, of course, paid for his services. His duties, however, should have kept him busy. They were:-

1) Not to receive aboard any convict whose health was suspect.

2) Examine each prisoner together with the medical officer of the hulk or prison from which the prisoner originated.

3) Inspect the convicts daily and determine that the diet was adequate.

4) Determine that the cleanliness and ventillation of the quarters aboard the ship were adequate.

5) Establish schools and conduct divine service each Sunday.

6) Establish and supervise exercise periods during the voyage.

The convicts themselves, after some years running the harsh gamut of Millbank, Pentonville, the hulks and holding prisons were usually glad to be going at last. Though often affected by diseases of some kind such as scurvy, dysentery, typhoid, typhus, smallpox, tuberculosis and numerous respiratory ailments they would lie liberally about their health or cover up with a long practised expertise.

Male Convict at Pentonville

The examinations were often hurried and slipshod, sometimes deliberately so. All prisoners had to have medical certificates from the shore authorities but often the latter would select first those they most wanted to get rid of. Irons were put on ulcerated legs so that stockings couldn't be taken off, but if the examining surgeon proved to be difficult the Inspector-General could step in and advise him that he must take certain men no matter what the problem appeared to be.

The system was ripe to be exploited in other ways. Though the rations were of good quality, if the surgeon did not supervise matters very closely the crew could cheat the convicts quite easily. Faulty weights and measures (usually hollowed out) were known to be held aboard some ships. The crews might later sell the excess in any ports of call en route, or upon final arrival.

Most surgeons were young, inexperienced and were not disposed to go into the convict messes. That was a daunting enough prospect for even the most hardened and experienced; and they were not aboard anyway to play brother's keeper, especially to a class of men well beneath them in the social strata of Victorian society. Most probably wished to reach the colonies as expeditiously as possible, with as few problems as possible. If two or three convicts died on the voyage that would have been within acceptable tolerances. Sometimes, undoubtedly, it was far easier to turn a blind eye and maintain a pleasant relationship with the captain for the duration of the voyage.

At embarkation each prisoner received a bed, pillow and blanket, two wooden bowls and a wooden spoon. The regulation dress was jackets and waistcoats of blue cloth, duck trousers, check or coarse linen shirts, yarn stockings and woollen caps - suitable for summer but quite inadequate for winter.

Each mess, of six or so convicts, received 20 lbs (9 Kgs) of bread, 12 lbs (5.4 Kgs) of flour, 16 lbs (7.2 Kgs) of beef, 6 lbs (2.7 Kgs) of pork, 1 lb (0.5 Kg) of butter, 8 ozs (0.25 Kg) of rice, 1.5 lbs (0.68 Kg) of suet, 3 lbs (1.4 Kgs) of raisins, 6 pints (3.4 litres) of oatmeal and 4 ozs (0.1 Kg) of sugar per week. Wine was issued occasionally. (1)

The members elected their own mess 'captains' who, in theory at least, were responsible for distribution of supplies, maintenance of tidiness and the orderly conduct within each mess. It very often didn't work out that way.

The prison quarters were in fact often dark and foul. In bad weather the scuttles (top covers) were closed and in the tropics the air was invariably stifling. Pitch dropped from seams and burned flesh. Two pints of water (often foul after weeks at sea) per man, per day was considered adequate.

The prisoners were kept busy sewing or knitting socks and schools were formed to teach basic literacy. Sometimes singing or dancing were allowed but more often gambling in the form of cards, dice or pitch and toss were the main pre-occupations. The main 'currency' was tobacco, for which men would often sell their personal effects (food and clothing) to gain a 'stake' for the next game.

For the exercise periods ladders were lowered to the 'tween decks and groups were brought up progressively, the more suspect being ironed together. They shuffled round and round the deck, with chains clanking, watched by wary guards on the poop deck.

ARRIVAL:

The Pyrenees arrived at Fremantle on the 30th April 1853, after a journey of 87 days. Aboard were 293 convicts (three died en route), 3 passengers, 29 male adult guards and 64 women and children. (2)

Before disembarkation the colonial surgeon and the port health officer would have conducted an inspection and after issuing a clean bill of health the Principal Superintendent of Convicts, or his representative, would have boarded for an inspection on behalf of the contractors - the Home Office. In the case of the Pyrenees no comment about the fate of the three convicts who died on the outward voyage is recorded in official documents.

During the inspection the convicts had an opportunity for complaint but one wonders how much it would have been in their interests to do so. At anchorage individual papers were brought up to date with details such as:

      1) Offences
      2) Sentences
      3) Date and place of conviction
      4) Trades
      5) Personal description
      6) Conduct report by surgeon-superintendent (3)

All the convicts who came to Western Australia were under 45 years of age and classified as being in good health. Half of each sentence had already been served and all were men with supposed good conduct records. It had been agreed that no Irish convicts should be sent, nor female offenders.

On arrival it was made clear to the convicts that unacceptable behaviour would result in 12 months in irons. A ticket-of-leave would only be issued when a prisoner had clearly shown he was able to live honestly. The men were searched, washed, given fresh clothing (a jacket, vest, trousers, socks, flannel and cotton shirts, boots, handkerchiefs and a hat. The first issue was free), medically examined and given a 'close' haircut. Their personal particulars were entered in the comprehensive convict register.

By 1851 many convicts had qualified for tickets of leave, which meant they were free to hire themselves out to colonists who were anxious for their services.

Once the prison superintendent had satisfied himself that a 'ticket' could be issued the recipient was interviewed by the chaplain. He then went to the Commissariat store and was given:

1. Bed and bedding (4 blankets)	6. A jacket
2. One pair of trousers	7. A hat
3. Four pairs of socks	8. Four handkerchiefs
4. Four cotton shirts	9. A pair of boots
5. A waistcoat	10. A belt

He was given sufficient rations to reach his allocated hiring depot (South Fremantle, Mount Eliza, Guildford, York, Toodyay, Bunbury, Albany or Port Gregory). It was estimated, for example, that five days was a reasonable time to travel to Guildford from Fremantle.

Returning to the Superintendent's office he signed the account book and acknowledged payment of any monies owing to him from gratuities or private cash. Then a pass was issued to him to proceed to his destination.

It was also made clear at this point that he was required to pay back his passage money in full before a conditional pardon would be granted. A man with a seven year sentence was required to pay back seven pounds, ten shillings; a ten year man's debt was ten pounds and a fifteen year man owed fifteen pounds.

The sum owed had to be paid back at a minimum rate of five pounds per year with quarterly payments to paid to the Commissariat storekeeper of the area he was in at the time. Considering that the average wage at the time was around twelve pounds per annum for a labourer the requirement was a heavy one.

The conditions imposed on the Ticket of Leave men were stringent and yet don't appear unreasonable. Governor Fitzgerald (1848-58) was not a harsh disciplinarian and did not appear to favour extremes of punishment, or indeed any excesses of treatment, by the convict administration.

The conditions of Ticket of Leave were:

1) The ticket holder was required to report to the Resident Magistrate within seven days of arrival in the district.

2) He had to report also within the first two weeks of January and June of each year.

3) Any changes of employment or residence had to be reported within seven days.

4) They were not permitted on ships without authority.

5) They were not permitted to run a hotel.

6) They were only allowed to stay in a town on a special pass (it seems they were required to stay out in the bush, out of sight and out of the way as much as possible).

7) They could not carry firearms without permission.

8) They were subject to a curfew when the bell was rung (usually at the police station at ten o'clock).

Each man, however, was free to choose his master and had to be paid a minimum of ten pound eight shillings with food and lodgings provided. Skilled men could and did, depending on demand, command much more.

A seven year man had to serve an 18 month minimum period on 'ticket' while a 10 year man had 2 years before he could apply for a Conditional Pardon.

Ticket of Leave men were free (and encouraged) to bring out their families on payment of half fare but, strangely, very few took advantage of the scheme and in the majority of cases wives and families did not join their families in the Colony.

Certainly the overall scheme was not without problems and recourse to the whip, the triangle and shackles is recorded. But the advantages must have been thought neglible because a public meeting in June, 1853 opposed the cessation of transportation when it was thought that the Home Government was thinking of doing away with the scheme or making substantial changes to it.

Many in the Swan River community felt that though, in principle, the process was distasteful and a taint on the colony, the hard, cold realities of their economic situation demanded a continuation. "The increase in the number of people and the large amount of money distributed by the penal department provided both the market for local produce and the means to pay for it, so that .... the whole colony seemed to have been roused from its state of lethargy and gave every promise of rapid advancement." (4)

Joseph Johns was allocated the Western Australian convict number of 1790. Going through before him was Archibald McIntyre (1789), a seven year man; a little way behind was George Clarke (1794), one of the unfortunates who was subsequently admitted to the Fremantle Lunatic Asylum. (5)

It had originally been laid down that men had to work for at least fifteen months on public works before being eligible to apply for a Ticket of Leave. The complement of convicts from the Pyrenees were more fortunate. The labour shortage in the colony was so critical that all of them were given immediate tickets and sent off to their allotted hiring depots with rations, clothing and passes.

For the time being then we lose track of Johns. From what we learn of him later it seems probable that he went to Guildford and from there to the Toodyay area. Less than two years later he was granted a Conditional Pardon on the 10th March, 1855. It meant then he was virtually a free man four years short of his original ten year sentence. We know therefore that he repaid his passage money and had no offences recorded against his name after arriving in the colony. He had now complete freedom of movement and full citizenship rights (such as they were for a former convict).

It should have been the end of his association with the penal system. But the real saga was yet to begin.

"CONVICT UNIFORM IN WESTERN AUSTRALIA

Nearly 10,000 male convicts (no women) were transported from Britain to Western Australia between 1850 and 1868. they served out their sentences here for the next 30 years.

Except for food, the convicts were almost totally supplied from England. Their uniforms were made in the tailor shops of the big London prisons in three standard sizes and sent out in annual despatches. Ordinary prisoners, ticket of leave men and men on special punishment on the chain gang wore different issues of clothing, which they received twice a year for summer and winter.

Broad Arrow Marks

The broad arrow mark signified British Government property. Sometimes the broad arrow was accompanied by the letters 'WD' for 'War Department', 'C & M' for 'Clothing and Munitions', and 'B O' for "Board of Ordnance'. These were the various government offices which supplied common uniforms (called 'slops') for the lowest ranks of the army and navy as well as for convicts.

Chain ganger in black and yellow suit, blue shirt, brown felt hat

The various marks were stamped in black ink on light-coloured fabrics and in white on dark fabrics. Sometimes they were small (only 2 cm long), few and discreetly placed inside the clothing. However, they were also used large (6 cm) and liberally scattered, any which way up, all over the pieces of uniform.

Ordinary Prisoners

The winter uniform was made of coarse dark grey woollen fabric. It comprised a jacket with six buttons of black metal or brown bone and a small stand-up collar, which could be rolled over to form revers; a waistcoat, also with buttons and stand-up collar; and trousers cut loose and straight with a buttoned fly. These were worn with a shirt of blue serge or flannel; a blue checked cotton neckerchief; a squashy felt hat with a medium wide brim; woollen socks; black boots; and a leather belt.

For summer the uniform was made of duck (fine unbleached canvas), dowlas (strong calico) or drabbet (dull brown linen). Shirts were of red or blue striped cotton, to be worn with the same neckerchief.

If engaged in messy work, the convict wore a smock made of duck or dowlas. This was just above knee length, long-sleeved, gathered at the shoulders but probably without any elaborate smocking. Convicts working on the pilot boats were issued with oilskin coats and hats

Ticket of Leave Men

Men working on a ticket of leave (provisional release) could buy their own clothes if they wished. It seems that many would buy personal 'best' clothes, but continued to take the government issue for work clothing. This was basically the same as the ordinary prisoners' uniform, but worn with a blue cloth cap with a leather peak (like a modern police cap) and a black neckerchief of better quality fabric.

Chain Gangers

Men sentenced to work in iron leg chains wore a bizarre particoloured uniform for extra punishment. It comprised the same basic pieces and cut as the ordinary outfit, but was made of coarse wool in black and bright mustard yellow halves. Thus the right hand front half of each piece was black and the left half yellow; it was reversed on the back and the collar.

Because the punishing iron chains remained on the prisoner's legs 24 hours a day, the sides of the trousers buttoned up (and could be unbuttoned) like a fly. the shirt, neckerchief, hat and boots were probably the same as the ordinary uniform.

The Preservation of Convict Uniform

Just five pieces of original convict uniform survive in Western Australia. They are in the collections of the WA Museum and the Fremantle Prison Museum. Because these historic pieces of clothing are fragile and irreplaceable thay are not on permanent display. Their survival represents one of the most intimate links we have today with the experience of the convicts of Western Australia."

(from Western Australian Museum Information Sheet, "CONVICT UNIFORM IN WESTERN AUSTRALIA")

CHAPTER THREE:

The Convict Era - 1850 to 1868

Problems and Parliamentary Reform:

The decade following the introduction of convicts in Western Australia saw something of a transformation in the colony. "The stagnant settlement of 1850 had become in ten years a hive of industry, a change which colonists believed to be wholly due to the introduction of convicts." (1)

Far from wanting to phase out the use of convicts ten years after their introduction many of the settlers were anxious to keep up the supply. But there were difficulties.

In 1861 the Duke of Newcastle (Secretary of State for the Colonies) was forced to reply to the W.A. Legislative Council that, " ... while the Imperial Government recognised the importance to the colony of an adequate supply of forced labour, a difficulty was created by the limited number of men who were being sentenced to periods of imprisonment sufficiently lengthy to admit of transportation." (2)

This might seem to suggest that society in England had changed dramatically for the better and that therefore fewer malefactors were coming before the courts. This was far from the truth. What in fact had happened was that agitators for social and penal reform were influencing policy makers at Westminster and a series of reforms were progressively enacted through parliament in the 1850s.

Chartists Riots – Newport, 1839.

New penal laws in 1853 and 1857 had wide sweeping effects. No longer would a man who had stolen a loaf of bread be transported; the statutes that provided for felons to be hung for a wide range of trivial offences were also eliminated.

Charity and compassion for the suffering of the lower orders were at last creeping into the consciences of the legislators and the men who wielded power within the community. The long battle, started, in part, by the Luddites, the Tolpuddle Martyrs and the Scottish Jacobins, organisations like the Chartists and the Prison Reform Society, and individuals like John Howard and Elizabeth Fry, was beginning to transform the social attitudes of centuries.

The upper classes and the privileged were listening and heeding. The revolt in the American colonies in 1775 had startled many and helped set in motion a social revolution in Europe. Writers, social reformers and philosophers like Montesquieu, David Hume, Benjamin Franklin, Tom Paine, Adam Smith, Voltaire and Rousseau were greatly influencing the thinking of many in Europe, particularly the newly emerging and influential 'bourgeoisie'.

Nobody wanted a repeat of the French Revolution in England. That frightening series of events had not been very far away across the channel and very few years had passed since. The lessons were apparent.

And so the parliament in London, often unwillingly, began to take long awaited remedial steps.

Unfortunately for Western Australia it now meant that a convict who had been handed down a seven year sentence, instead of being merely a petty thief as the 1850 convict usually was, might now conceivably be a practised criminal with quite serious offences on his charge sheet.

".... Captain Henderson (the Comptroller-General of Convicts) stated in 1856, the English prison authorities were sending out 'the men they do not hang'. The joint committee appointed in 1862 also affirmed that 'it has been shown that in one case the Governor of Chatham Prison was specially instructed to select for embarkation the convicts least fit to be discharged at home'." (3)

The quality of convict landing in W.A. by 1860, then, had deteriorated. The colonists tended to blame Governor Kennedy and accused his 'casual' administration. They may have been right in part. Indeed in the early 1860s the benign policies of Colonel Henderson, Comptroller-General of Convicts, might not have been stringent enough for the 'harder' breed of transportee now arriving.

In the early 1850s Henderson had intimated that the convicts deserved better treatment than those who had earlier been sent to N.S.W. and Tasmania. He acted with compassion, tolerance and understanding. It was regarded as an enlightened point of view by some but seen by others as bordering on the heretical. Even Governor Fitzgerald did not always agree with him.

Nevertheless by the time Henderson went home on sick leave in 1856 he had set up an administration that gave the newly arrived convict every chance to succeed and assimilate in the new environment.

When Henderson returned in 1858 he introduced a system of incentives for prisoners enabling them to accumulate, through industry and education, credits toward a ticket of leave. He reduced punishments to a minimun and established in the main convict establishment a library and a school. (4) The prisoners commonly called it 'the college'. (5)

Henderson's "..... underlying principle was remedial - to reform the prisoners and to offer him every inducement to once more become a respected member of society. That it was hardly penal is quite evident." (6)

Fremantle Prison
Early watercolours of the Prison – by Captain H. Wray

It was an enlightened approach for the 1850s. But from around 1860 onward it proved inappropriate for many of the 'new breed' of convict. The problem was compounded within the colony by the increasing numbers of colonial prisoners, freemen and emancipists who were of poor quality and persisted in troublemaking.

It seems likely that Dr John Stephen Hampton was brought from Tasmania to replace Kennedy as governor with a specific purpose in mind - to 'tighten up'. A former Comptroller-General of Convicts in Tasmania, Hampton was known to be a strict disciplinarian and a capable administrator.

He first came to Australia as a ship's surgeon on the "Constant", arriving in Van Diemen's Land in 1843. Eventually he was appointed to the post of Comptroller-General on the island. In 1855 however he was ordered to appear before a select committee to answer questions on his methods of administration. It was alleged that he had derived profit from the mis-use of convict labour. Hampton handled the crisis by simply refusing to appear before the committee.

No harm seems to have come to his career even though he was acknowledged as being tyrannical and harsh (the 'white overseer'). He utilised convict labour to its fullest extent and pursued a program of public works with considerable energy. (7)

He came to Western Australia ".... with a notorious reputation from his stint in charge of the convict establishment in Tasmania. 'An opportunist and self-seeker not moved by any finer feeling,' wrote a contemporary from Tasmania, the Reverend Rogers. The superintendent of Fremantle prison, Lefroy, wrote, '.... Our present Governor Hampton is not at all to my liking. Although he walks around this prison, attended by me, once a week, I have never once exchanged a friendly thought or sentence with him." (8)

There were indications that Dr Hampton's particular approach in Western Australia was sorely needed. A commission of enquiry set up in 1862, looking into the whole question of transportation and penal servitude reported: ".... that a very dangerous element had .... been sent out was apparent ....." (9)

Later in the year the Home Government decided to abolish the transportation system altogether but no definite date was given. It wasn't until the early months of 1865 that ".... the House of Commons was informed that the system would come to an end in three years time ...." (10)

When the news was announced the debate among the colonists was fairly evenly divided with probably most weight supporting the cessation.
".... many colonists felt they could no longer derive further benefit from convicts, while the presence of them debarred the colony from a fuller voice in the management of its own affairs." (11)

Perhaps it is mere co-incidence that Edmund Henderson resigned in 1862 and left the colony for England in the following year. There is every good reason to suppose though that the harsher penal methods required by Governor Hampton were anathema to him and the two men conceivably did not see 'eye to eye'.

In England Lieutenant-Colonel Henderson sold his commission and was appointed Surveyor-General of Prisons and Inspector-General of Military Prisons. Six years later he became Chief Commissioner of Metropolitan Police and during his fifteen years of control the force was re-organised and expanded considerably. The C.I.D. (Criminal Investigation Department) was also set up. In 1878 he was created K.C.B.. He died in London at 75 years of age.

Sir Edmund Henderson was not only a capable administrator and an accomplished engineer, but he was a man it seems who knew and understood men, a valuable assett when handling those who stepped ashore at the Swan River Colony only weeks out of the atrocious and often sub-human conditions of the prisons, hulks and transports of the English penal system. For the twelve years of his tenure in W.A. he gave the convicts every chance to turn their backs on their former lives and start afresh. He could be a stern disciplinarian but was most often just and fair. "That convicts have not left a permanent smear on the face of W.A. is due in no small measure to him." (12)

Colonel Edmund Henderson

Captain Newland arrived on the 14th January, 1863 to take over the position of Comptroller-General of Convicts from Henderson. From the outset he was at odds with Governor Hampton. It was to be a difficult period.

Hampton re-instituted many of the methods used in Tasmania - the whip, chain gangs and excessive solitary confinement. He worked the convicts relentlessly on a programme of building and construction. A roadway was completed between Perth and Fremantle using blocks of jarrah wood (called 'Hampton's cheeses'), the completion of the new parliament house was pushed ahead, pensioner barracks were built, as was a causeway to the east of Perth and a bridge over the river at Fremantle. The Perth Town Hall is another outstanding example of the drive of John Hampton and his use of convict labour.

In the early years of his administration the colonists appeared to be generally well pleased with their governor. Captain Newland was not. He resigned and went back to England early in 1866. In the interim, to fill the gap, Governor Hampton appointed his son, George, as the Acting Comptroller-General of Convicts.

George Hampton already held the post of the governor's private secretary (at one hundred and fifty pounds per annum, plus a clerk), the clerk of the Council (two hundred pounds p.a.) and clerk to the Board of Finance (one hundred pounds p.a.). In all (the Comptroller-General's job included), Hampton Junior's total annual salary was in the vicinity of twelve hundred pounds per annum (when a skilled worker could expect a wage of around fifty pounds).

Mr George E. Hampton

There were cries of protest. It was felt that George had no particular qualification or talent to fit him for the new position. To add further insult to injury it was then learned that he was to draw the Comptroller-General's one hundred pounds lodging allowance while in fact still living at Government House. Disaffection from certain quarters is best portrayed in this caustic editorial in the Perth Gazette (May 4th, 1866):-

"This appointment surprises no one, as by all who had any acquaintance with the character and disposition of His Excellency, it had been anticipated that such would follow the success attending the long course of discourtesy, insult and bullying by which Captain Newland was driven from his office. But, until the disgraceful affair had been fully completed there were some persons who, still retaining a degree of respect toward Governor Hampton, as Her Majesty's representative, yet had hope that he would have sufficient regard for his own honour and that of his office, as not to sully it by such an abuse of patronage as must alienate from him that last slender portion of confidence which they placed in his sense of right and justice.

And who is Mr George E. Hampton? We will enlighten the public a little. He is the Governor's son, Private Secretary, Clerk of the Council and Clerk to the Board of Finance, and he has acted as general overlooker and spy about the Government offices, for which we are not aware he has drawn any pay, unless it be from the "secret information" fund of the Police Department ...... his conduct and supercillious demeanour, had rendered himself the object of dislike and contempt to every gentleman with whom he has come in contact .... is there a single individual in the community who relishes such a prospect, who does not feel dismay that any share in the destiny of the colony should fall into the hands of such a person as we all know Mr George Hampton to be? We very much doubt there is.

...... no honest and conscientious man can overlook but with disgust upon such an unscrupulous open-faced piece of jobbery, as the appointment of a man to an office from which it is notorious his and his father's treatment has just driven an officer and a gentleman away.

.... Governor Hampton ... so conscious that it would be disapproved of here as well as in England, that up to the minute of the notice of appointment being given to the department, he had not informed a single person of his purpose, not a member of the Executive was consulted, and the delay in the appointment after the departure of Captain Newland was evidently for the purpose of stealing a mail upon the home authorities."

If the Gazette is to be believed, even in part, it was indeed high-handed behaviour from Governor Hampton.

But the governor appeared to take little heed of public opinion or the advice of his council. He carried out what he saw fit with almost total arrogance, in private affairs as well as in public.

He disapproved of the hymns sung in the cathedral and suggested to the Anglican Bishop of Perth, Mathew Hale, the selections that he would like. Hale was not impressed and said so, in no uncertain terms it seems. Thereafter the Governor, his family and retinue worshipped in a chapel specially set up at Government House - no doubt to the chagrin of the Bishop.

Hale responded by criticising the morals of the Hampton family and in particular pointed to the affair George was reputed to be having with one Mrs Young. In June, 1866 the Bishop also sent a written statement to Downing Street condemning Hampton Junior and his insolent behaviour.(13)

In 1858 Hale had set up the first school in the colony and had successfully applied for a grant from the Legislative Council to help defray the expenses. Governor Hampton stopped the grant and directed that the funds go to the Catholic Church to help them in the erection of their new cathedral. The Bishop's school was forced to close.

But Hampton fell out with the Roman Catholic church too. They rejected a provision of the 1863 divorce law and the governor retaliated by refusing to allow convicts to quarry stone for a North Fremantle orphanage despite the fact that the Sisters were working voluntarily for destitute children, hitherto kept at public expense. (14)

The alienation of influential people like Bishop Hale was probably not enough to damage the Governor's credibility too much. In a small community it was probably regarded by some as good entertainment.

What happened within the realms of the convict administration was very much more serious. It sent a flood of complaints to the Secretary of State for the Colonies and was certainly taken very seriously by the Home Office.

George Hampton did indeed seem to have little of the talent necessary to deal with the type of people within the confines of the Fremantle Convict Establishment. "..... the efficiency of the system suffered under his control and the convicts chaffed more under the restraint.
Attempted escapes became more numerous ..." (15)

"....during the eight months ending March, 1867, over 90 attempts at escape were recorded - more than three times the number of any previous period of the same length." (16)

During the six years of the Hampton administration a total of 6599 strokes were awarded to 96 convicts in the triangles. (17) The newspapers, of course, took great delight in announcing these facts.

'In a humourous vein one convict wrote to the Home Office stating that, "I would recommend the government to superannuate Governor Hampton for his past colonial service, and either buy or purchase him an estate in the neighbourhood of Lake Eyre."' (18)

Whipping Post

Also around this time Joseph Johns, the convict ironworker from Wales, had been making news. The Perth Gazette reported on March the 15th 1867:-

"Probably no event in the colony ever more tickled the visible faculties of the public than did the escape of the notorious convict, 'Moondyne Joe' on the afternoon of Thursday last week. Much of the amusement felt arose from remembrances of the theatrical exhibition made of Joe by the Acting Comptroller-General (George Hampton) when he was last captured - chaining him to a post in one of the yards, and Mr Hampton improving the occasion by addressing the assembled prisoners and pointing out to them Joe's sad condition as an example of what would befall them if they went and did likewise .....

..... the Superintendent could not believe it and brought forward a theory that it could not possibly be a fact; however the alarm bell was rung; the gun (cannon) was fired and the police and military distributed, and an express sent to Perth, which is said to have greatly disturbed His Excellency and Mrs Hampton's digestion at dinner ...... he then offered a reward of twenty pounds from his private purse (!) if Johns was brought in DEAD or ALIVE."

Johns had in fact surfaced again at Toodyay in 1862 on a charge of horse stealing. Over the next five years or so he had made a series of escapes from gaols and work parties. He had proved to be so much of a nuisance that George Hampton, during his term as Acting Comptroller-General built a special cell for him and was reputed to have been so confident of keeping Johns behind bars at last that he boasted openly that if the prisoner managed to escape he would grant a free pardon. Johns duly escaped.

There were howls of mirth throughout the colony. The Hamptons had 'egg on their faces'. The legend of Joseph Johns, better known as Moondyne Joe, was made. Dr John and George Hampton contributed to its fabric every bit as much as Joe. It was a story that appealed to all, especially in those days when a far wider gulf existed between working men and the upper echelons within government and propertied circles. Joe had 'put one over' them. In an isolated part of the world where the downtrodden had little to enthuse about a hero had sprung into being.

But the popular press were not the only ones to villify the governor and his son. The Secretary of State admonished Dr Hampton when he heard of the affair and had his own appointee take up office as quickly as possible. The new Comptroller-General, Mr Wakefield, took up the reigns in May, 1867 and began to re-implement as many of Lieutenant-Colonel Henderson's former methods as was possible.

Some colonists wanted the transportation of convicts to continue despite the Home Office's earlier directive. The York Agricultural Society, one of the bodies who strongly petitioned for the introduction of the system originally, envisaged a gloomy future for the colony when transportation ceased. "The cessation of transportation is at present the stoppage of nearly the only source from which the labour market is supplied." (19) But there was little chance of retention of the system in W.A., particularly after the Hampton administration.

The last convict ship, the "Hougoumont", arrived on the 10th June 1868, with 75 convicts aboard, many of them Fenians, political prisoners of the Irish Republican Brotherhood, six of whom were to make an indelible mark on the history of W.A. with a spectacular escape from the colony on the American whaler, "Catalpa" in 1876.

When the Home Office first suggested to Governor Hampton in 1867 that the Irishmen be sent to Western Australia he " .... rejected the proposal saying that with a strong Irish element among the people and with three-fifths of the military force also of Irish birth he feared the consequences if Fenians were gaoled at Fremantle." (20)

".... He refused to have them as it would only draw upon the colony an American raid to liberate them, and he had no means to resist it .... they will surely attempt to rescue these men by bombarding Fremantle, knocking down the prison walls and letting six hundred ruffians loose to pillage and plunder the town and commit all sorts of atrocities. There is no attempt too daring or too vile for these Fenians ....." (21)

As it transpired the Governor's fears proved groundless. Apart from relatively minor incidences they gave little trouble. He wrote in August 1868: "I am now able to report with real satisfaction that their conduct .... has with the exception of two or three cases of a very trivial nature been most exemplary, and that they are deserving of high praise for real obedience and willing industry... " (22)

The fact remained though that most Fenians had a burning desire to leave the colony by one means or another and return to the help 'the cause'. As time went on they became more restive and a series of incidences, including a minor mutiny in 1869, eventually lead to the Catalpa escapade.

But at the end of 1868 when transportation finally ended the number of men still under the control of the convict administration was 3158. A total of 9721 had been transported to Western Australia since 1850. (23)

The term of Dr John Stephen Hampton as Governor of W.A., also finished in 1868. The 'tyrant' left and the dismantling of the system could begin in earnest. It would be twenty years or so, though, before the Home Office in Britain handed the responsibility over entirely to the Western Australian Government.

Governor John Stephen Hampton left a strong imprint on the history of Western Australia. He was a larger than life character. It seems most colonists either admired him or hated him. There doesn't seem to have been an appreciable middle ground.

Governor John S. Hampton

A scroll (24) presented to him by prominent citizens of Perth just before he left portrays one side of the coin:-

---

" To:
HIS EXCELLENCY JOHN STEPHEN HAMPTON,

Governor and Commander in Chief

in and over

The Colony of Western Australia and its
Dependencies and Vice Admiral of the Same.

We the under signed Inhabitants of the City of Perth, cannot allow Your Excellency to retire from among us without expressing our high appreciation of the great zeal, ability, and unwearied industry with which you have administered the Government of this Colony during more than six years.

Whilst the great public works that you leave behind will be monuments of your practical judgement, the deep interest which you have ever taken in all that relates to the substantial advancement of the Colony, as well as the urbanity evinced by Your Excellency, and Mrs Hampton, in presiding over the hospitalities of Government House, must leave in our memories pleasing recollections of your administration.

We cannot conclude this brief expression of our feeling without heartily wishing Mrs Hampton that restoration to health which is usually expected to attend a return to one's native land. But whether there, or in whatever other locality it may be the lot of both of you to sojourn , we very sincerely hope that the blessings of life may surround your habitation."

There follows six ordered columns comprising 186 signatures of members of the Perth establishment of 1868.

But the Perth Inquirer found these eulogies, including one which had compared the former governor, Sir Arthur Kennedy, unfavourably against Dr John Hampton, hard to stomach.

In its September 18, 1868 issue it reported, in part:

"....nor would he (Kennedy) have tried to wreak his impotent wrath upon the clergy because a high-minded conscientious divine like the Bishop (Hale) found it necessary to rebuke bare-faced indecency when it dared to outrage and affront public propriety ..... Men the most unfit for their office were not selected merely from the predilections of their patron.

We are a long suffering people and accustomed to submit in silence to insults from those who have the power to insult us, but we cannot bring ourselves to consent to subscribe to statements altogether false and without a shadow of foundation. We cannot be made to believe, and only contemptible sycophants will be found to assert, that any honour has been reflected on this colony by the appointment which is happily about to terminate.

Let not the injudicious critics of the INQUIRER force us to recount the real merits of the passing administration or we shall take such a review of acts and conduct as will make the English people wonder at the complaisance (sic) of Australian settlers who are treated to the grossest indignities by inferior minds, and then (make) addresses expressive of their admiration and gratitude."

There is little doubt, from the evidence we have before us today, that Dr John Hampton achieved much in his six years as governor of Western Australia. What is also apparent is the questionable and sometimes distastful way he went about achieving his purposes.

"His administration could hardly be described as peaceful, and there is no doubt that much of the public criticism of it was justified. His interference into matters relating to the convicts, his tyrannical methods toward them, and his action in appointing his son to the position of Acting Comptroller-General of Convicts were strongly, and without doubt justly, resented.

There certainly was not equally good ground for accusing him of delaying the inauguration of representative government, though it is questionable whether he would have urged it had not the force of public opinion become too strong to be resisted. There was one phase of his administration, however that was eminently successful - that of the erection of public works. More than any previous Governor he applied himself to meet the needs of the settlers in that direction, and many public buildings still in use bear testimony to the success of his efforts.

He used convict labour largely for these purposes, it is true; but after all, Western Australia was entitled to any benefit she might receive from that labour as some return for consenting to allow the incubus of a criminal population to rest upon her. On the whole the benefits he conferred were lasting in nature, while his mistakes were ephemeral." (25)

But what we don't often recognise is the toll public office takes, even on those with apparent thick skins. When John Hampton left the colony he was not a completely well man and he had little time left to enjoy his retirement. He died toward the end of 1869, at Hastings in England, at the age of 59 years. (26) The six years in Western Australia had extracted a heavy toll.

1868 heralded the end of an era for Britain and Australia, not only in penal history, but in a social and moral imbalance that had been in existence since perhaps 'the greater villain was let loose to take the common from the goose.'

A new era was dawning.

CHAPTER FOUR:

JOSEPH BOLITHO JOHNS - 1855 to 1900

The Avon River follows a broad valley through York and Northam until it reaches the West Toodyay region. There, in the vicinity of Cobbler Pool, the frowning sides of the valley crowd in as if to thwart any further intrusion.

From Cobbler Pool down to Walyunga and beyond, the river valley is narrow, sometimes hostile and conceivably dangerous to anyone careless enough to take it lightly. As such it is relatively untouched. The terrain is too precipitous for settlement, too rugged for much practical usage, even today.

But over a hundred years ago the West Toodyay valley played host to a small, thriving population which crept into its profusion of shadowy gullies and all but disappeared from the brutal outside world.

Many of them, 'old lags', cowed and brutalised from years in the English prisons or on the Thames hulks, bruised from the chains of work gangs or still shattered from their time in the detention closets deep within the bowels of sailing ships pitching wildly through towering seas, bodies sometimes broken and their minds and spirits still very much under siege, followed the stock route down-river past Cobbler Pool and were swallowed by the warm comforting embrace of Mother Earth.

They built rude shelters from branches and rocks and mud deep in the stands of jarrah and wandoo and blackboys; beside the massive grey strength of huge granite boulders. They caught possums, kangaroos and emus and to supplement their diet they 'duffed' a sheep or two from a passing mob summering on the grasses that were still luxuriant in the valley long after the feed had dried up and withered elsewhere.

Their clothing fell to pieces so they wore possum skin slippers and aboriginal 'boukas' or kangaroo skin capes. Their hair grew long and matted and unkempt. To the outside world they would have appeared half-starved, derelict and objects of scorn or pity. But for the men themselves the West Toodyay valley above Walyunga was, conceivably, something of a paradise.

For the first time in years, hungry as they might have been at times, they had what they'd dreamed of all along during the desperate months and years in the stinking bowels of a prison or the mind-numbing confusion and desperation of separate confinement. They had solitude, they had peace and quiet and they were no longer harried and bullied by crude officialdom - they were free. Free to lie in their rough bunks until late in the morning and let the calm and solitude of the bush wash around them. Here time could partly heal the deep wounds, although it is doubtful the tranquility of the bush would have entirely eradicated the scars imprinted on their minds and in their souls.

After his pardon was issued in 1855 it seems fairly certain that Joseph Johns, ex-convict number 1790, disappeared into the hills and was lost to officialdom and the world for some years.

But early in August 1861, Johns was apprehended in the Toodyay area and charged with stealing a horse. (1) Several days later he or an accomplice unscrewed the hinges from his cell door and he escaped. He took with him the horse in question and the resident magistate's new bridle and saddle. Later, deep in the bush, he destroyed all the evidence that could have been used to convict him.

He was re-captured and subsequently tried at the Supreme Court in Perth for prison breaking. Sentenced to three years penal servitude he was transferred to the Fremantle Convict Establishment and became colonial prisoner, number 5889. (2)

After seven months at Fremantle Johns was transferred to Perth on a work party for 15 months before he was discharged on ticket of leave on the 5th January 1864. His behaviour was apparently good and he posed no problems for the authorities. Perhaps he regarded it all as a 'fair cop' or under the Henderson regime the stringencies of serving a sentence were not particularly difficult.

On the 29th March 1865 Johns was this time charged with unlawfully killing an ox at Kelmscott. He was sentenced to penal servitude for ten years on the 5th July, 1865. (3) This time he strenuously protested his innocence.

Now lodged in Fremantle prison as colonial prisoner number 8189, the seeds of the Johns saga began to germinate. On the 1st of November 1865 he was placed on a work party to the Canning River and seven days later, in company with David Evans, he absconded.

The pair were on the run for nearly a month. They displayed great endurance and bushmanship and led the troopers and trackers on a long and exhausting chase. They were captured at Doodenanning and brought before the resident magistrate at York, Mr W. Cowan who chose to hear the case in York rather than send the pair on to Perth.

Surprisingly he gave them the comparatively light sentence of only twelve months in irons for their transgressions. Mr Cowan must have sympathised with their points of view, to a degree at least, and Joe's probable protestations of innocence over the original charge of killing an ox with felonious intent.

Mr Cowan subsequently placed a deposition before the governor on the matter. Dr Hampton, most often quite unmoved by similar representations, ordered a full report to be given on Johns and Evans when their term in irons had been completed. (4)

Magistrate's Residence, York

On the 10th April 1866 Johns was permitted to present a petition to the chief justice. The case must have been well presented. The matter was referred to the governor and Johns was awarded a four year remission from his sentence.

But despite this, inexplicably, Johns attempted to escape again in July 1866. He was caught and sentenced to six months in chains.

It seems something had snapped. Was it the new, far more stringent regime within the walls of the Fremantle establishment now - the oppressive nightmare of Pentonville all over again? Were the years of brutal and cynical disregard for his rights and feelings as a fellow human being adding up? Did he sense, inherent in the penal system, a monumental injustice? Was it just that he couldn't 'take it' any longer? Had he gone mad; an 'aberration of the mind'?

Only a matter of weeks later he succeeded in escaping again and this time picked up John James, Thomas Bugg and John Bassett from a work gang at Greenmount where the Darling Range rises abruptly from the coastal plain.

For around seven weeks this time "Moondyne Joe & Co." (as they were dubbed by the press) led the troopers a merry dance in and around the Toodyay hills and finally further inland. There is reason to believe that Joe was intent on building up his supplies while in the Toodyay area before making for the South Australian border. Joe's bushmanship and knowledge of police tactics were more than a match for the pursuers for quite a time. The foray was well thought out and may have succeeded with a little more luck.

The press followed the chase avidly and many working class people, convicts and 'old lags' cheered the escapers on. By this time Governor Hampton was beginning to make many enemies within the colony and Moondyne Joe became something of a focal point and a weapon to 'get back' at what many perceived as the high-handed arrogance of the colony's chief executive.

The party was finally apprehended at Bodallin Soak over two hundred miles east of Perth at the end of September, 1866.

Again York Resident Magistrate Cowan championed Joe's cause to George Hampton, the Acting Comptroller-General of Convicts. Hampton, Junior, was not moved by the letter in the least and is reputed to have described Johns as "an immense scoundrel". (5)

So Joe was chained by the neck in the prison yard and shown to the other convicts as an example. Naturally the press learned of it and weren't slow to turn the knives in the waning credibility of the Hamptons.

George Hampton had the prison carpenters make up a special cell for Johns which he boasted was escape proof. Very little light could get in and ventilation was poor. The comptroller was reputed to have boasted also that if the prisoner escaped this time he would grant him a pardon.

On March 7th 1867 Johns escaped. Using a clever ruse he dug his way under the prison wall and made his exit through the prison superintendent's yard in his underwear. The rest of his clothing had been left on a pick made up to represent a human figure at a prison yard rockpile. The prisoner had been put to work there during his mandatory exercise period away from the special cell.

It was nearly two years this time before the authorities were to catch up with him again.

The colony exploded with mirth. The press again played their part in whipping up anti- Hampton feeling:

> "Probably no event in the colony ever tickled the riseable fancies of the public than the escape of the notorious convict, Moondyne Joe, on the afternoon of Thursday last week. Much of the amusement felt arose from remembrance of the theatrical exhibition made of Joe by the Acting-Comptroller General when he was last captured - chaining him to a post in one of the yards and Mr Hampton improving the occasion by addressing the assembled prisoners and pointing out to them Joe's sad condition as an example of what would befall them if they went and did likewise.
>
> Joe's ingenuity in making his escape from his apparently hopeless condition has gained him many sympathisers who express an opinion that he has earned his freedom, ... " (6)

In the taverns, down the back alleys and increasingly out in the open a popular tune was adapted for the occasion:-

> "The Governor's son has got the pip,
> The Governor's got the measles,
> But Moondyne Joe's given them the slip,
> Pop goes the weasel." (7)

The Hamptons were not laughing. For the first time in the colony's history an order was given out that the absconder was to be taken, DEAD or ALIVE. (according to the 'Inquirer')

The Hamptons left the colony late in 1868 while Joe was still at large. The Moondyne Joe episode must have been a thorn in the side of a man who, his convict administration aside, had been a capable and effective manager of the colony for four years.

Johns was re-captured at "Houghton", in the Middle Swan area, on the 25th February 1869, while replenishing his stocks of wine in the cellars.

He was sentenced to an additional twelve months in irons, six months of that to be in separate confinement. A little later he was given three additional years in irons for breaking and entering at Houghton. In all it was to be about twenty five years before he would be free again.

But Joe was made of stern stuff. He petitioned, still claiming his original innocence. He eventually did receive some remission and finally in May 1871 he was released on Ticket of Leave to the Vasse. Comptroller-General Wakeford, Superintendent Lefroy and Governor Weld had apparently decided there was little point in keeping the man in perpetual incarceration until somewhere into the 1880s.

It would be a fitting end to report that after the wisdom and magnanimity shown by the authorities, Joseph Bolitho Johns stayed out of trouble and managed to rehabilitate himself within the free community. The fact of the matter is that he was gaoled again (for a month) in 1872 and for the rest of his life had minor offences recorded against him at intervals. None of the offences were of great significance and it seems he may have been regarded by the police as a nuisance rather than an outright villain.

His pardon came through in June 1873 and thereafter he worked in varying locations around the colony from Fremantle to Coolgardie and numerous locations between. It seems he never settled to a vocation for long and was something of an unsettled itinerant.

He married Louisa Hearn, the widowed daughter of a former navy warrant officer, in 1879. She died in 1893, probably from one of the epidemics that decimated the eastern goldfields at that time, although her death certificate merely states apoplexy. (8) There are no known descendants.

Joe returned to Perth eventually. He died at the Fremantle Lunatic Asylum on the 13th August, 1900 of senile dementia. (9) The records state he was 72 years of age. For some time his condition had been deteriorating and he had earlier in the year been committed for the treatment of a mental disorder. In the light of what he had been subjected to in his earlier years it doesn't seem surprising. Many men who had been through the same experiences either went insane or died at a much earlier age.

It is perhaps a tribute to Johns's toughness and resilience, or his sheer stubbornness, that he lasted long enough to see in the new century and the beginnings of a changing attitude to social justice and an equality which would eventually begin to regard all men as being equal, not just in the eye of God, but in the eyes of other men.

Joseph Bolitho Johns occupies a paupers' grave (number 580A) at the Fremantle Cemetery. With him are buried W. McGrath, S. Steel and R. Peck (a fellow convict).

On the granite stone covering the grave is a carving of handcuffs with a broken chain. Underneath is the Old Welsh word, "Rhyddid" which means FREEDOM.

CHAPTER FIVE:

CASE STUDIES

CONVICT - JOHN WILLIAMS (William Cross)

John Williams, the accomplice of Joseph Johns, adopted a psuedonym when he left his home area in the West Country of England and went in search of a job, or merely to eke a bare existence wherever he could. It was a common enough occurrence. Under the depressed social conditions of the time many of the working class either had to steal to survive or had adopted it as a natural way of life - it was better than starving and, for some, preferable to working for a pittance under appalling conditions.

If caught under an assumed name and address they would be tried in the locality of their given address rather than in their true home area where the stigma and disgrace among friends and families would probably have been traumatic for all concerned.

Williams adopted a false name and was in fact far from his true home when apprehended. Originally he was from Horseley in Gloucester (1) but had left to either look for work or easier 'pickings'. He secured a job as a canal boatman and was very probably ferrying produce through the canal system which served the ironworks at Clydach in central Wales.

Brecon Canal and Tramway

He was apprehended under the name of William Cross, together with Johns, near Chepstow, on the 15th November, 1848. It wasn't until the 23rd March, 1849 however that they were brought before the Lent Assizes at Brecon charged with: "... illegally entering the premises of Mr Richard Price, Esquire, of Pentwyn Clydach ... and from there taking three loaves of bread, one piece of bacon, several cheeses, a kettle and a quantity of salt."(2)

From the newspaper report of the trial the pair pleaded not guilty and conducted an unexpectedly long and spirited defence, casting doubts on the evidence of the prosecuting sergeant and so casting aspersions on the validity of detail brought by the prosecuting counsel. (3)

It was to no avail. Both were convicted and sentenced to ten years transportation despite the fact that Johns was purportedly a minor and had no previous convictions. It is interesting to note that in several previous cases that day other prisoners had been brought before the same court on very similar charges, pleaded guilty and had received sentences ranging from three weeks to three months imprisonment. Those cases had been dispensed with in minutes.

Brecon Courthouse

Were Williams and Johns unwise to plead not guilty? It didn't pay, perhaps, to hold up the pressing business of the court and in so doing perhaps annoy the judge - in this case a knight of the realm, Sir William Erle.

It is interesting to note, too, the composition of the jury. Almost without exception the twenty one members sworn in at the commencement of proceedings that day were men of position and property in the surrounding community. (4) Two were members of parliament and many of the others had the term "esquire" appended after their names (the dictionary describes an esquire as belonging to the order of English gentry ranking next below a knight).

The English legal system prides itself on the fact that a trial by jury is, in the final analysis, a judgement by one's peers. In the trial of Williams and Johns it seems that it would hardly have been the case. The gulf was too wide. Their crude speech, mannerisms and rough clothing would hardly have earned them any sympathy from among those who were of the same class as Mr Richard Price, Esquire, the owner of the farmhouse into which Johns and Williams were accused of breaking. Arguably their fate was sealed as soon as they opened their mouths to defend themselves.

The pair were lodged in a local prison and it was not until the 23rd October, 1849 that they were taken to London and lodged in Millbank prison pending their removal to Pentonville.

John Williams lasted the mandatory twelve months separate confinement in Pentonville prison and then in December, 1850 he was taken to Dartmoor Prison in Devon, some fifteen miles north of Plymouth.

Dartmoor had originally been a military prison built to house French and Americans captured in England's earlier wars. Now it was being extended and converted to cater for the growing ranks of the enemy within.

Williams would have been re-united with Johns again when Joe was transferred from light duties at the Shorncliffe army establishment in October, 1851.

John Williams was put aboard the "Fairlie" in March, 1852, at Plymouth. He arrived at Hobart on the 4th July.

The Tasmanian convict register for new arrivals records Williams as being five feet four inches tall (163 cms), fresh complexioned with a large head. He had brown hair, black whiskers, oval visage (Johns had a 'piercing' visage), a medium forehead, black eyebrows, dark eyes and medium nose, mouth and chin. There were various tattoos on his arms (ships, a lark and a 'foulanchor').

We can follow Williams/Cross's early career in the colony by the string of petty transgressions recorded against him in the register. Several times he absconded while on ticket of leave and on a more noteable occasion he received six months hard labour (September, 1854) for being ".... discovered .... upon the females premises without authority and holding communication with a female servant."

He had his ticket of leave revoked on several occasions and was probably lucky not to be sent to Port Arthur to serve further periods of separate confinement in the building specially erected to duplicate the new Millbank and, later, the Pentonville models in London.

He eventually received a conditional pardon on the 11th of December, 1855, but it must have been revoked because another was awarded to him at a later date.

On the 18th July, 1859 he is recorded as having received his Certificate of Freedom. Thereafter there are no more entries in the convict register and no trace of him in civil documents.

One would hope that despite his harrowing experiences at Pentonville and in the various gaols in England, he managed to rehabilitate himself. Unfortunately the skant evidence we have seems to suggest he may have been one of the lonely, shiftless men who lived out their lives in abject poverty and degredation, ejected by their own country, a victim of forces beyond their control, then rejected and demeaned by the new society into which they were brusquely thrust. The forgotten men we have preferred to sweep under our historical carpet.

The verses below may very well serve as an epitaph for John Williams and the many others like him:

"From distant climes o'er widespread seas we came
Though not with much e'clat or beat of drum,
True patriots all, for be it understood,
We left our country for our country's good!"
No private views disgraced our generous zeal,
 What urged our travels was our country's weal;
And none will doubt but that our emigration
Has proved most useful to the British nation."

(Attributed to Henry Carter, 'celebrated' pickpocket, from the first convict play performed in Australia, "The Revenge")

Convicts - WILLIAM GENTLE & WILLIAM PALMER

The story of William Gentle, Swan River Colony convict number 7113, is also a study in courage. Unlike Johns, though, he bore his fate with a silent stoicism and it seems never at any time did the authorities have to record any mark of misconduct against him.

His passage through the prison system was, if anything, far more testing than that suffered by most other convicts, Johns included. That he survived at all is remarkable; that he achieved a pardon 13 years after his trial and went on to build a new life for himself and his family is extraordinary. His descendents today have good reason to regard this man with awe as they work the lands that he first took up and farmed over one hundred years ago.

It began near Cambridge, England in 1851. He and a friend, William Palmer, were put on trial on the 19th March for breaking and entering the house of Sarah Rich, widow of Harlton, and stealing from her stays and pocket, money to the value of upwards of twenty pounds ($40).

Gentle protested his innocence all along and even after the jury had returned a verdict of guilty he felt strongly enough to protest to the judge. But in the words of the court reporter: ".... after some severe comments ... (the judge) .... sentenced the prisoner to transportation for life." (5)

It was probably unfortunate for Gentle and Palmer that immediately prior to their hearing the same judge had heard cases against three other men who had been accused of malicious wounding to cause bodily harm. This trio received life sentences.

After a mandatory period of separate confinement Gentle and Palmer were placed aboard the "Ascendent" bound for Bermuda. En route two hundred Irish prisoners were picked up from Cork. These men were regarded as the 'lowest' of types. It wasn't a reputation lightly earned. Prisoners from Ireland weren't noted for their easy acceptance of any form of British authority. They were treated accordingly. Being 'lumped' in with them Palmer and Gentle, in all probability, would have suffered similarly.

The British had a large fleet stationed at Bermuda. Convicts were used for the building of docks and allied facilities, and for the daily running and maintenance of the station.

Gentle and Palmer were placed aboard the hulk, "Coromendal" at Ireland Island. (6) Battened down below in the tropical heat with men who had been originally sentenced to death for crimes against the crown ranging from murder, arson, highway robbery, horse and cattle stealing, attacks on police barracks etc., the day to day fight for life began.

"..... rations were ill-adapted to the climate, periodical outbreaks of dysentery were responsible for many deaths, and scurvy also took a heavy toll of the prisoners. In addition ophthalmia, due to the glare of the sea on the limestone rocks, would cause men to stumble and fall as they walked even along a straight and smooth path. But the worst scourge which flayed Bermuda was West Indian yellow fever, carrying off hundreds of victims in the course of its many visitations. The worst epidemic was in 1853 when 160 convicts lost their lives and a far greater number were permanently broken in health." (7)

The hulks themselves, grounded in thick mud and housing a crowd of ill-fed and depressed men, formed excellent centres for its (yellow fever) dissemination.

A fine contemporary painting (1857) by Le Marchant, of the Hulk DROMEDARY, which was sent to Bermuda in 1826, being the second Hulk to be used to accommodate convicts working on the Dockyard Defences. Hulk is shown alongside the short arm of the North yard. In the background is the Victualling Hulk ROYAL OAK.

Attempted escapes were frequent, attempted murders, brutality, vice and corruption were almost everyday occurrences from which Gentle and Palmer had to find refuge the best way they could.

Punishments by the lash, the yoke and in the black hole were part and parcel of one's existence. Trade in rum aboard the hulks brought frequent rioting and violence on some noteable occasions. There is no doubt that of all the hulks in the history of the system the Bermudan ones were the worst.

William Gentle and William Palmer survived this hell for nine and a half years.

In 1857 the hulks were abolished in England. It was not until some time later (1862) that the Bermudan hulks were finally broken up.

In April, 1861 Gentle and Palmer were put aboard the "Medway" for transferrence back to England. On the 30th September they were at Chatham the naval base toward the mouth of the Thames (8), where C.F. Newland, later a Comptroller-General of Convicts in Western Australia, was in charge. Gentle was prisoner number 4008; Palmer number 4002.

Chatham Naval Dockyards – Convicts Excavating a Large Basin

William Palmer was sent to the Swan River Colony in the "Norwood" and arrived on the 9th June 1862. Early in 1863 Gentle was placed aboard the "Clyde" at Chatham. The ship reached Fremantle on the 29th May 1863.

The convict register describes Gentle as being a little over 5' 6" tall (170cms), with brown hair, blue eyes and a dark complexion. His viseage was 'long', his appearance was middling stout and he had a scar on his left cheek. He was a labourer by trade and was married with two children. (9)

On the 23rd June 1863 (only a little over three weeks after he arrived), William Gentle, now 36 years of age, was granted his Ticket of Leave. He moved to York and worked on farms north of the town.

On the 15th February, 1864 Gentle gained his Conditional Pardon. (10) Four months later Ann Gentle, his wife, arrived aboard the "Strathmore" with children, Samuel and Rebecca and son-in-law, John Endersby.

The re-united family moved to the Quellington area twelve miles north-east of York, firstly leasing crown land and later buying it and extending their holdings over the years until they (the Gentles and Endersbys) became some of the largest landholders in that district.

William Palmer gained his Ticket of Leave on the 23rd of September 1862 but was not granted his Conditional Pardon until the 14th of June 1864. He too moved to the York area as a farm labourer and one assumes he kept up his association with William Gentle. One would hope that the friendship which had helped both withstand pressures few men have had the misfortune to have undergone, would have remained firm.

In one register entry Palmer is recorded as having a wife in England. Shipping records do not show that she ever came to the colony. One hopes therefore that Palmer would have had a privileged place at the hearth of the Gentle homestead whenever he visited. It is not known, definitely, where or when he died.

William Gentle died on the 5th November 1890, at the age of 65 years, and was buried in the York cemetery. The inscription on his tombstone bears mute testimony to the difficulties he suffered even the amid the success of his later life:

> "Affliction sore long time he bore
> Physicians were in vain
> Till God of love took him above
> And erased him of his pain."

It seems he had not entirely been able to put the Bermuda hulks behind him.

The Gentle family still farm at Quellington today on the original holdings that William Gentle took up soon after being granted his pardon.

FOOTNOTE:

In 1908 William Gentle's grandaughter, Mary Endersby married William Llewellyn Hitchcock, grandson of pensioner guard, Jeremiah Woolhouse, at a grand ceremony in the Anglican church on the "Tipperay" property of one of the major landholders in the state, Mr W. Burges. (11)

It was scarcely a decade and a half since William Gentle, convict, and a former labourer on the property of Burges, had died. Under no circumstances, at that time, would a man in his lowly position have been allowed to set foot in that church. Now, his family, respected members of the landholding 'squattocracy', were welcome.

A vigorous mobility, unheard of in the 'Old Country", was afoot in the new land.

CHAPTER SIX:

HERITAGE

For eighty of the two hundred years of our history, thieves, forgers, arsonists, murderers and political agitators were transported here, 'out of sight, out of mind'. At the end of the first 40 years of settlement in New South Wales the ratio of convict, ex-convict and 'currency man' (Australian born) to free settlers was seven to one. In a country's formative years that must have been no small influence. What effect has it had? What then has the convict phenomenon contributed to the nation of Australia?

"If the convict influence was strong in early Australia, what was its particular nature? Undoubtedly the brutality of the prison system and harshness of life in the colony re-inforced many vicious aspects of convict behaviour, but the same conditions also fostered traits usually regarded as characteristic of the convicts in this country: a collective and anti-authoritarian morality, physical endurance and resourcefulness. Added to these germinal elements of the Australian mystique was the greater degree of social mobility occurring in comparison with older societies which, combined with the insatiable demand for labour, tended to have a generally levelling effect without diminishing class consciousness and hostility." (1)

It is obvious that the convicts helped to break and bring to heel an often harsh, hostile and unforgiving environment. In the case of Western Australia, in particular, it could be argued that importation of convict labour, albeit unwillingly, brought the struggling colony back from the brink of disaster. Free settlers alone could not manage it. The convicts were indispensable.

Men like William Gentle survived the living hell of the Bermudan hulks and became the raw material from which succeeding generations drew resilience, strength and courage in the face of great odds. From such pioneers came sons and grandsons who were tough, hardy, resourceful and independent. In the 1915-18 conflict these qualities were translated from the bush to the slopes of Gallipoli, the wells of Beersheba and to the Somme in France and Passchendaele in Belgium.

The Anzacs took the glory in the first World War but the foundations on which their legends stand were, in many cases, laid in the bowels of a convict hulk, or a generation or two later, wrestling hundreds of miles inland with the hostility of the Australian landscape.

From Mary Gilmore's "Old Botany Bay" might well come the true epitaph of William Gentle and the thousands of others like him:-

> "I was the conscript
> Sent to hell
> To make the desert
> The living well.
>
> I split the rock
> I felled the tree
> The nation was
> Because of me."

Of course the opposite may well have been true in Tasmania. The island might have progressed without the de-stabilising influence of the convicts in a landscape more forgiving than the west of the continent. Certainly the near anarchy existing on the island after the death of Lieutenant-Colonel Collins held back progress for some time.

But a more important question seems to be, not so much what role the convict has played in shaping the landscape, but the part he has played in influencing the way Australians regard people and events today - in other words, attitudes. Is it here that the most powerful legacy lies, for better and for worse?

Ned Kelly has been described as: "....that loud-mouthed, law-breaking, swaggering son of an Irish convict ...." (2) Most in authority at the time would have agreed whole-heartedly.

Ned was brought up at his mother's knee learning considerable predjudices against British authority and the way it was administered. But, unlike his parents, he was a native-born Australian and had little of the fears and awe that they might have felt. He was a bushman - a superb rider, a crack shot and had the supreme confidence in himself that only comes of challenging and beating adversaries (the authorities or the bush) on numerous occasions. And deep down a sense of injustice boiled. He was not alone. Thousands of others had a similar fire simmering in their belly.

"To lower class people generally - and usually to themselves only - bushrangers were "wild colonial boys":- Australians par excellence. In a newly developing society which lacked war heroes it was not surprising that ' .... folk tradition clothed their crimes in nationalistic garb.' " (3)

"The (small) selectors of north-east Victoria, discerning a note of social protest in his (Ned's) actions, viewed him more as a noble robber or Robin Hood than as a common criminal." (4)

It isn't necessary to relate the Ned Kelly story here . But what can be said is that Ned, like Ben Hall the Wheogo small landholder in New South Wales, Mathew Brady the 'Robin Hood' of Van Dieman's Land and Joseph Johns the resourceful, stubborn Welsh miner in Western Australia, came to represent a vital part of the fight, not so much against corrupt police and officialdom, but against the shackles of social oppression which had afflicted the 'working' man since he was forced off the common land in Britain where he'd been relatively content with his tiny cottage and a few sheep and ducks.

The common labourer was flung then, by circumstance, into the destitution and the slums that accompanied the Industrial Revolution in England - and there left to make do, or to rot. That legacy and its backlash is still with us today. There is probably something of an inevitability about it. Labour and union movements abound. Some say the tail now wags the dog. In view of what the dog has done to the tail over the last two centuries it is hardly surprising. Arguably it has been a predictable swing of the historical pendulum.

Ned Kelly's life was short (he was hanged at 25) but he gave impetus to a wave that perhaps started around the time of Eureka and probably waned after the drive toward Federation. To paraphrase Angus McIntyre, "Ned's seeming daring and invulnerability appealed to the vulnerable - the small selector enduring hardship (Ned's mother), struggling against the land, the squatters and the authorities." (5)

Is it here that we can glimpse an insight into a sizable portion of the Australian psyche and character?

Dr Russell Ward in "The Australian Legend" says the Australian pastoral worker was: ".... a practical man, rough and ready in his manners, and quick to decry affectation ... He is a great improviser .... willing to 'have a go' at anything, but .... content with a task done in a way which is 'near enough'. Though capable of great exertion in an emergency, he normally feels no impulse to work hard .... He swears hard and consistently, gambles heavily and often, and drinks deeply on occasion .... He is usually taciturn .... stoical .... and sceptical about the value of religion, and of intellectual and cultural pursuits generally. He believes that Jack is not only as good as his master, but .... probably a good deal better, and so he is a great 'knocker' of eminent people, unless, as is the case of his sporting heroes, they are distinguished by physical prowess."

He is a fiercely independent person who hates officiousness and authority - especially when .... embodied in military offices and policemen. Yet he is very hospitable and, above all, will stick to his mates through thick and thin .... He tends to be a rolling stone, highly suspect if he should chance to gather much moss." (6)

Is this the man we still see in the 'pub' on any Friday night through the length and breadth of Australia?

BEN HALL   NED KELLY

How many of these characteristics can be attributed to the circumstances of 100 - 150 years ago? We had then an oppressed majority, vehement in their condemnation of those in authority and yet, inherently, in awe of them. Perhaps today's 'tall poppy' syndrome is consistent with this. A pronounced social equality in this country has brought many more opportunities to make good - but beware a man climb too high (and attempt to leave the brotherhood)!

So, then, does a confusion therefore still exist within our nationalistic make-up? On the one hand the convict heritage gave us a strong urge to be independent and distinctly Australian, personified in the poetry of Henry Lawson:

> "Sons of the South, awake, arise!
> Sons of the South, and do.
> Banish from under your bonny skies
> Those old world errors and wrongs and lies
> Making a hell in paradise
> That belongs to your sons and you ...."

But deeply ingrained too is the conservative element - the desire to be considered valid on the world stage. Is this why we went back to the 'apron strings' in 1914? To a 'mother' who had treated us with a haughty indifference and disdain for a century and a quarter?

Was it just that we were anxious to flex our new found muscle, our spirit? Had we progressed far enough by 1914 to begin to look for a wider acceptance?

We went to Gallipoli and France and much of our lifeblood drained away in foreign soil in a conflict few truly understood past the lust for adventure and a vague notion that the Empire was in peril. Was blood thicker than water after all? Did the ghosts of those whose tortured minds survived Pentonville or wielded a 'pike' at Eureka turn in their graves?

And so, as Lawson prophesied in "The Roaring Days", the demands of wars, politics and international and domestic commerce brought us back to the mainstream:

> ".... Those golden days have vanished,
> And altered is the scene;
> The diggings are deserted,
> The camping grounds are green;
> The flaunting flag of progress
> Is in the west unfurled,
> The mighty bush with iron rails
> Is tethered to the world."

Lawson regretted the advent of the railway line and saw clearly what it would do to our hard-won individuality, an independence that had taken root in a sub-soil of which the convict experience made up a great part.

There were those however who wished fervently it hadn't occurred at all. J.S. Battye wrote in 1923: ".... there does exist the fact that Western Australian history has been tainted by a convict period - and no material prosperity that ensued at the time will ever efface the stain. At that price all that accrued was dearly purchased." (7)

Over 60 years later that pained statement appears now to be faintly absurd. The quirks of historical perspective have made us proud of the toughness, forbearance and durability displayed under almost intolerable burdens of physical and emotional tyranny. The modern viewpoint has stripped away the predjudices and we now call the convicts simply, pioneers. They are at least the equal of the early free colonists. In many ways they bore the greater burden in the forging of the nation. Perhaps Dr Battye would change his view now too as the twentieth century draws to a close and with time and longer hindsight our perspectives have changed.

When only yesterday we had tight clamps on the cupboard door for fear of the skeleton's rattle, today we are actively looking for the remnants of our heritage. And so we should. It is probably a sign of a growing maturity. Time has lifted the carpet corners and we've found there's nothing to hide anymore. Indeed there are fascinating new insights to gain by sifting through the forgotten particles of dust.

It seems there's a new confidence. Perhaps, therefore, we won't much longer be so dependent on the tenuous crutch of the bushman/Anzac legend - a hastily constructed edifice atop a too tall pedestal on a makeshift base?

Will April the 25th eventually be supplanted, or joined, by December the 3rd (Eureka Stockade - 1854); or January the 26th (Phillip raises the flag at Sydney Cove - 1788); or the 21st of September (the beginning of the counterattack against the Japanese on the Kokoda Trail - 1942; more truly our finest and most necessary military 'hour' according to many)?

Where is the balance? We are probably too young as a nation to have struck a 'happy medium' between the radicalism of our early years and the conservative demands of modern internationalism. The ancient Greeks inscribed on the walls of the temple at Delphi: "Know Thyself". We are probably only part way along that particular path.

It seems important,however, that whatever refinements come to smooth the sharp edges of the rough diamond, the convict heritage must be nurtured as an integral part of our national metamorphosis; the scars of the lash, the stark terror of the darkened cells of Pentonville, the vile stench of the rotting bowels of the hulks and, perhaps most importantly, the arrogant indifference of those that had the power to condemn other men to a purgatory on earth, should not be forgotten or allowed to fade. There are lessons to learn even now. And from ingredients like these, vitality is added to our history and our heritage.

The ghosts of the convicts must play a part.

REFERENCES:

PROLOGUE:

(1) J.S Battye, "WESTERN AUSTRALIA" (Facsimile Edition),
     - University of Western Australia, Perth, 1978, p. 127

(2) Ibid, page 128.

(3) Ibid, page 197.

(4) Perth Gazette (newspaper) 17 April, 1847.

(5) J.S. Battye, page 202

(6) Ibid, page 203.

(7) Ibid, page 204.

(8) Ibid, page 207.

Chapter One:

(1) Cardiff & Merthyr Guardian (newspaper), 31 March, 1849.

(2)   Meurig Evans, "CHILDREN in the MINES",
     National Museum of Wales, Cardiff, 1979.

(3) MACQUARIE Dictionary.

(4) P. Priestley, "VICTORIAN PRISON LIVES",
     Methuen, London, 1985, p. 29

(5) D. Ritchie, 'The Voice of Our Exiles'; or 'Stray Leaves
     From a Convict Ship', Menzies, Edinburgh.

(6) Priestley, p. 37

(7) Ibid, p. 34

(8) Pentonville Register, P. Comms (pp 64-70), P.R.O., Kew, London.

(9) Priestley, page 38.

(10) Ibid, Introduction

(11) Pentonville Register, P. Comms (pp 64-70), P.R.O., Kew.

(12) Prison Registers, H.O. 8, P.R.O., Kew.

(13) S. Taylor, in T. Stannage (Ed) "CONVICTISM IN WESTERN AUSTRALIA", U.W.A. Press, Perth, 1981, p. 28

(14) W.S. Branch-Johnson, "THE ENGLISH PRISON HULKS", Christopher Johnson, London, 1957.

(15) Ibid.

(16) Louis Garneray, quoted from "ENGLISH PRISON HULKS", Chapter 7.

(17) Reverend J.M. Guilding, Ibid.

(18) Branch-Johnson, p 25

Chapter Two:

(1) Charles Bateson, "THE CONVICT SHIPS", Brown, Son and Ferguson.

(2) From the W.A. ALMANAC (Battye Library, Perth).

(3) Charles Bateson

(4) Battye, p. 209

(5) W.A. Convict Records, Battye Library, Perth.

Chapter Three:

(1) Battye, p 240

(2) Ibid, page 246.

(3) Ibid, page 464.

(4) Allan Hale, WEST AUSTRALIAN NEWSPAPER, November/December, 1976.

(5) Battye, page 460

(6) Ibid, page 464.

(7) J.S. Battye, "CYCLOPEDIA OF W.A.".

(8) G.Russo and H. Schmitt, "SWAN RIVER MANIA", page 58.

(9) J.S. Battye, "WESTERN AUSTRALIA", U.W.A. Press, p 248

(10) Ibid, page 250.

(11) Ibid, page 250.

(12) Ibid, page 253.

(13) Perth Gazette, 18 September, 1868, page 2.

(14   Ibid.

(15) Battye, page 254

(16) Perth Gazette, 22 March, 1867.

(17) Barry Boyd, "GOVERNOR HAMPTON", Graylands Teachers
     College Thesis, Battye Library, Perth.

(18) Russo and Schmitt, page 58.

(19) From C. Gertzel, Minutes of York Agricultural Society
     Annual Report, 28 October, 1868, "The Convict System
     in Western Australia, 1850-70", U.W.A. Thesis, Battye Libray, Perth.

(20) Rica Erickson, "THE BRAND ON HIS COAT", University of Western
     Australia Press, Perth, 1983, p.116

(21) Ibid, page 117.

(22) Ibid, page 136.

(23) Battye, Appendix III

(24) Hampton Papers (MN 623, ACC 2528A), Battye Library, Perth.

(25) Battye, page 279.

(26) Australian Biographical Index, Battye Library, Perth.

Chapter Four:
(1)   Police Records, (ACC 129), Battye Library, Perth.

(2)   Convict Records, Battye Library, Perth.

(3)   Perth Gazette, 7 July, 1865.

(4)   quoted from Ian Elliot, "MOONDYNE JOE, THE MAN AND THE
      MYTH", U.W.A. PRESS, Perth, 1978.

(5)   Ibid.

(6)   Perth Gazette and W.A. Times, 15 March, 1867

(7)   Quoted from: Ian Elliot, "MOONDYNE JOE, THE MAN AND THE MYTH".

(8)   Death Certificate no. 442/1893, W.A. Registrar General, Perth

(9)   Death Certificate no. 983/1900, W.A. Registrar General, Perth.

Chapter Five:
(1)   Convict Records, Tasmanian State Archives, Hobart

(2)   Trial Report, "The Welshman" newspaper, 30 March, 1849.

(3)   Trial Report, "Cardiff and Merthyr Times", 31 March, 1849

(4)   Assize Records, "P. Comms" 76, No 2, P.R.O., London.

(5)   From: "THE Cambridge Chronicle and University Journal, Isle of Ely Herald
       and Huntingdonshire Gazette, March 29, 1851

(6)   Prison Register (H.O. 8), Public Records Office, Kew.

(7)   W.S. Branch-Johnson, "THE ENGLISH PRISON HULKS", Chapter 18

(8)   Prison Register (H.O. 8, No 149), P.R.O., Kew.

(9)   Convict Records (ACC 1156, Register R 26), Battye Library, Perth.

(10)   Rica Erickson, "DICTIONARY OF WESTERN AUSTRALIANS, 1850-68" (Vol 2),
       U.W.A. Press, Perth, page 206

(11)   YORK CHRONICLE newspaper, June, 1908, Battye Library, Perth.

Chapter Six:
(1)   Eleanor Hodges, p 5, in John Carroll, "INTRUDERS IN THE BUSH", OXFORD,
       Melbourne, 1982.

(2)   Angus McIntyre, Ibid, page 38.

(3)   Hodges, Ibid, page 10.

(4)   McIntyre, Ibid, page 38.

(5)   Ibid, page 52.

(6)   Russell Ward, from Eleanor Hodges, Ibid, p.3

(7)   J.S. Battye, "WESTERN AUSTRALIA"

BIBLIOGRAPHY:

England and Europe:

"THE VILLAGE LABOURER", J. & B. Hammond, LONGMANS.

"THE TOWN LABOURER, 1760-1832", Ibid.

"THE ANTI-SOCIETY", Kellow Chesney, GAMBIT.

"VICTORIAN PRISON LIVES", Phillip Priestley, METHUEN.

"THE CONVICT SHIPS", Charles Bateson, BROWN, SON & FERGUSON

"THE ENGLISH PRISON HULKS", W.S. Branch-Johnson, CHRISTOPHER JOHNSON.

"CONVICTS AND THE COLONIES", A.G.L. Shaw, FABER & FABER.

"THE CRIMINAL PRISONS OF LONDON AND SCENES OF PRISON LIFE",
Henry Mayhew and John Binney - GRIFFIN.

"CHILDREN IN THE MINES", R. Meurig Evans, NATIONAL MUSEUM
of WALES.

"CHILDREN IN THE IRON INDUSTRY", Ibid.

"DARTMOOR PRISON", Rufus Endle, BOSSINEY BOOKS.

"LIFE IN WALES", A.H. Dodd, B.T. BATSFORD Ltd.

"THE PATTERN OF PAST INDUSTRY", J. Van Laun, BRECON BEACONS
NATIONAL PARK COMMITTEE.

"THE CLYDACH IRON WORKS AND THE ECONOMIC AND LABOUR PROBLEMS
WHICH CONTRIBUTED TO ITS DECLINE", Colin M. James, PRIVATE
THESIS.

"BRECKNOCK AND ABERVAGENNY AND MONMOUTHSHIRE CANALS",
R. Alan Stevens, GOOSE & SON.

"THE FATAL SHORE", Robert Hughes, COLLINS HARVILL, London,
1987.

"POLICE and PRISONS", P.F. Speed, LONGMANS, London, 1970

Australian -

"TRANSPORTED: IN PLACE OF DEATH", Christopher Sweeney, MACMILLAN.

"A PICTORIAL HISTORY OF BUSHRANGERS", Tom Prior, Bill Wannan, H. Nunn, HAMLYN.

"INTRUDERS IN THE BUSH", Editor: John Carroll (Ed.), OXFORD.

"SHADOW OVER TASMANIA", Coultman Smith, J. WALCH & SONS, HOBART.

"THE FATAL SHORE", Robert Hughes, COLLINS HARVILL, London, 1987.

Western Australian

"A HISTORY OF COMMERCE AND INDUSTRY IN WESTERN AUSTRALIA", Peter Firkins (Ed), UNIVERSITY of W.A..

"WESTERN AUSTRALIA: A HISTORY FROM ITS DISCOVERY TO THE INAUGURATION OF THE COMMONWEALTH" (Facsimile Edition), J.S. Battye, U.W.A. PRESS.

"THE STORY OF THE SWAN DISTRICTS", Canon A. Burton, BURTON.

"OLD TOODYAY AND NEWCASTLE", Rica Erickson, TOODYAY SHIRE COUNCIL.

"THE BRAND ON HIS COAT", Ibid, U.W.A. PRESS.

"DICTIONARY OF WESTERN AUSTRALIA" (Volumes 2 & 3), U.W.A Press

"THEY WISHED UPON A STAR", P.T. McMahon.

"MOONDYNE JOE - THE MAN AND THE MYTH", Ian Elliot, U.W.A. PRESS.

"ECONOMIC ASPECTS OF TRANSPORTATION TO W.A.", P. Anderson, U.W.A. THESIS.

"BEHIND THE LIGHTHOUSE", M.C. Carroll, IOWA STATE UNIVERSITY Ph.D THESIS (contained in the Battye Library).

"THE CONVICT SYSTEM IN W.A., 1850-70", C. Gertzell, U.W.A. THESIS (Battye Library).

"THE STORY OF A HUNDRED YEARS", H. Colebatch.

"A CRITICAL EXAMINATION OF TRANSPORTATION TO W.A., 1849-68", Allan D. Gooch - W.A. TEACHERS HIGHER CERTIFICATE THESIS, Battye Library, Perth.

"GOVERNOR HAMPTON", Barry Boyd, GRAYLANDS TEACHERS COLLEGE THESIS (Battye Library).

"MOONDYNE", J.B. O'Reilly, P.J. KENNEDY, New York.

"JAMES STIRLING", Alexandra Hasluck, OXFORD.

"SWAN RIVER MANIA", G. Russo and H. Schmitt - Lynwood Enterprises Pty Ltd, 1987.

PICTORIAL ACKNOWLEDGEMENTS:

Page 5:   Convict Hulk, "York" - Mansell Collection.

Page 8:   Ball and Chain - courtesy Ansett Airlines and JMA Ogilvy & Mather (artist, Malcolm Lindsay)

Page 12:   from R.Meurig Evans, "Children in the Mines, 1840 to 1842", page 17,National Museum of Wales, 1979.

Page 14:   from Mayhew and Binney, "The Criminal Prisons of London etc."

Page 16:   Ibid

Page 17:   Ibid

Page 19:   Ibid

Page 21:   Ibid

Page 22:   Ibid

Page 23:   Ibid

Page 25:   Ibid

Page 34:   Fremantle Prison, courtesy Art Gallery of Western Australia

Page 36:   Edmund Henderson, from Speed, P.F., 'Police andPrisons', Longmans, London, 1968.

Page 37:   Pictorial Collection, Battye Library, Perth.

Page 39:   Whipping Post, Mayhew and Binney

Page 42:   Pictorial Collection, Battye Library, Perth.

Page 47:   Photo W.J. Edgar.

Page 51:   Ibid

Page 52:   Michael Blackmore, from "The Patterns of Past Industry in the (Brecon Beacons) National Park", National Park Committee, 1976.

Page 53:   Dewi Davies, "Brecknock Historian", D.G. & A.S. Evans, 1977.

Page 55:   Plough Gang - National Library of Australia, Canberra.

Page 57:   "Dromedary Hulk", courtesy Bermudan Archives.

Page 58:   Chatham, from Geo. Bidwell, "Forging His Chains", Harford, Conneticut, 1888.

Page 63:   'Ned' - "Australasian Sketcher", July 31, 1880. 'Ben' - Municipal Library, Forbes, N.S.W.

Page 65:   Courtesy, Fremantle Prison Museum.